THE HEART'S DOMINION

WHERE SPIRIT, MIND, AND BODY BECOME ONE IN GOD'S GLORY

Discovering the Sacred Intelligence That Rules from Within

Minister Joyce Toney

Copyright Page

© 2025 Joyce Toney. All rights reserved.

ISBN:979-8-9936149-2-2

Published by **YESICAN Ministries / GOD'S DESIGN4YOU INC.**

bhbp@yesican77.com   www.yesican77.com

Scripture quotations are taken from the **Amplified Bible (AMP)** unless otherwise noted.

No portion of this book may be reproduced or transmitted in any form without prior written permission of the publisher, except for brief quotations used in reviews or educational materials.

Printed in the United States of America.

TABLE OF CONTENTS

DEDICATION 1

ACKNOWLEDGMENT 2

INTRODUCTION 3

CHAPTER ONE
    The Hidden Brain Within the Heart 5

CHAPTER TWO
    God's View: Man Looks Outward, God Looks Within........................ 12

CHAPTER THREE
    The Heart as a House of Authority... 18

CHAPTER FOUR
    The Hebraic Meaning of *Levah*: A Dwelling for Divine Rule 24

CHAPTER FIVE
    The Glory Field: Energy, Presence, and Spiritual Emission 30

CHAPTER SIX
    The Heart That Rules the Mind 36

CHAPTER SEVEN
    Guarding the Gate of Your Inner House.. 42

CHAPTER EIGHT
When Authority Is Surrendered: How the Enemy Fills the Heart 48

CHAPTER NINE
The Language of the Heart: How God Speaks from Within 54

CHAPTER TEN
When the Heart and Spirit Agree: The Power of Inner Covenant 61

CHAPTER ELEVEN
The Frequency of Faith: How the Heart Transmits Belief into Reality 67

CHAPTER TWELVE
The Battle of Frequencies: When Faith Meets Fear 73

CHAPTER THIRTEEN
The Rhythm of Peace: Living in Divine Coherence 79

CHAPTER FOURTEEN
The Anatomy of Wholeness: When Spirit, Mind, and Body Heal as One 85

CHAPTER FIFTEEN
The Healing Intelligence of the Heart: How God's Spirit Regenerates Life from Within 91

CHAPTER SIXTEEN
The Electromagnetic Signature of Glory: How God's Energy Marks and Protects the Believer 97

CHAPTER SEVENTEEN

The Heart as a Portal of Light: Bridging Heaven and Earth Within .. 103

CHAPTER EIGHTEEN

The Magnetic Field of Love: Drawing Miracles, People, and Purpose into Divine Alignment 109

CHAPTER NINETEEN

The Energy of Forgiveness: Releasing the Past and Restoring Spiritual Flow 115

CHAPTER TWENTY

The Heart's Dominion Restored: Walking in Wholeness, Authority, and Light.. 124

Dedication

To all who seek wholeness of spirit, mind, and body through the indwelling presence of God.

May your heart become the dwelling place of His glory, your mind renewed by His truth, and your body a vessel through which His power flows to heal the world.

Acknowledgment

All glory and honor belong to the Eternal King, who placed within me the burden and the beauty of this message. To the Holy Spirit — my Teacher and Comforter — who guided every word and turned revelation into illumination.

My deep gratitude to the faithful partners of YESICAN Ministries, mentors, and intercessors who have prayed, believed, and labored for the manifestation of God's purpose in the earth. To every reader whose heart longs for transformation — you are the reason this work exists.

May this book ignite a revelation of the divine order that heals the whole person and releases the glory of God through you.

Introduction

When the Heart Thinks Before the Mind

We live in a world that celebrates intellect yet often ignores the intelligence of the heart. Modern science has only begun to discover what the Word of God declared thousands of years ago — that the heart is not merely a pump of blood, but a center of divine perception, governance, and life.

In 1991, research in neuroradiology revealed that the human heart contains approximately 40,000 neurons that communicate with the brain and the body. Scripture had already said, "As a man thinketh in his heart, so is he." (Proverbs 23:7) The scientist calls it "bio-electrical communication"; the Kingdom calls it **revelation in motion**.

From Genesis to Revelation, God has been after the heart. The Lord does not measure a person by outer appearance but by the hidden counsel of the heart (1 Samuel 16:7). It is within the heart that faith is conceived, truth is born, and glory is released. When the heart is aligned with the Spirit of God, the mind is renewed and the body becomes a living instrument of healing and worship.

This book invites you into a journey of divine alignment — where Spirit, Mind, and Body become one through the dominion of a surrendered heart. We will uncover the spiritual science of the heart's brain, learn how the glory of God is transmitted through your inner being, and receive biblical principles that govern emotional, mental, and physical healing.

Every chapter is a revelation and a practical pathway toward wholeness. You will be challenged to see your heart not as a metaphor but as a living sanctuary — a dwelling place where God's Spirit merges with your spirit to govern your thoughts, your choices, and your health.

When your heart rules with righteousness, your mind thinks with clarity, and your body responds in harmony. This is the Kingdom pattern of divine dominion — a life where the heart is not divided, the soul is not tormented, and the body is not bound.

So prepare yourself to listen not only with your mind but with your heart. Let each page be a mirror that reveals the condition of your inner house and a doorway through which God's glory can enter. As you read, may your heart become the place where Spirit, Mind, and Body are made one in Him.

CHAPTER ONE

The Hidden Brain Within the Heart

"For as a man thinketh in his heart, so is he." – Proverbs 23:7

Part A — Revelation and Definition

Before there was ever a study in neuroscience, the Creator had already written within our being a design so profound that even the most brilliant minds still marvel at its mystery. God created the **heart as the command center of the whole person**—the seat of authority where spirit, mind, and body find their alignment and direction.

The *brain of the heart* is not a poetic idea; it is a spiritual and physiological reality. In 1991, scientists confirmed that the human heart contains more than **40,000 sensory neurons**, capable of learning, remembering, and making decisions independently of the cranial brain. These findings describe what Scripture has revealed all along: **the heart thinks, feels, and governs**.

When the Bible says, *"As a man thinketh in his heart, so is he,"* it unveils the truth that thought does not originate in the mind alone—it is born in the heart and transmitted to the brain. The mind executes what the heart believes.

Definition of the Heart's Brain

The Heart's Brain is *the inner governing intelligence of the human being, designed by God to process divine truth, regulate emotional and physical responses, and manifest the life of the Spirit through the body.*

It is both biological and spiritual—housing electrical, magnetic, and energetic dimensions that mirror the unseen realm of God's power.

In simple form:

- The **spirit** receives revelation from God.
- The **heart** interprets and believes it.
- The **mind** translates belief into understanding and action.
- The **body** manifests the outcome of that belief.

This is divine order. When the heart is out of alignment—when fear, bitterness, or unbelief dwell there—the spirit's revelation is distorted, the mind becomes double-minded, and the body reflects sickness, fatigue, or dis-ease. But when the heart is pure and yielded, it releases an electromagnetic field stronger than the brain's—*a measurable signal of life and peace*—which Scripture calls **the glory of God**.

Part B — Spiritual Clarity and Kingdom Revelation

God designed the heart as a **house of authority**. In Hebrew, the word *levah* (heart) is formed from two ancient letters: **Lamed**, meaning *shepherd's staff or authority*, and **Beth**, meaning *house or dwelling*. Combined, they reveal the heart as *a dwelling place of divine authority*.

The heart, therefore, is not simply a physical organ—it is a **spiritual sanctuary** divided between human will and divine indwelling. In one chamber, man decides; in the other, God reigns. The condition of the heart determines which authority governs the whole being.

When we submit the heart's dominion to God, the Spirit merges His life with ours. The result is *oneness*—the unity of spirit, mind, and body functioning as one Kingdom instrument. The brain in the head receives instruction, but the **brain in the heart issues the command.** This is why Jesus said, *"Blessed are the pure in heart, for they shall see God."* Purity of heart restores divine perception, allowing the believer to sense God's presence, think His thoughts, and embody His will.

The heart is also the **seat of conscience.** Romans 2:15 teaches that the law of God is written upon the heart. When that law is defiled, conscience becomes dull and the mind drifts into confusion. But when the heart is washed and renewed, conscience awakens and spiritual intelligence increases. This is the process of sanctification—the continual cleansing of the heart so that the mind may be transformed and the body may serve as a living testimony of health and holiness.

When a person says, *"My heart is heavy,"* heaven hears a cry from the seat of government within that soul. That inner weight is evidence of misplaced authority—where pain or fear has taken the throne meant for peace and trust. Yet God promises: *"A new heart I will give you, and a new spirit I will put within you."* (Ezekiel 36:26)

This is not repair but **recreation.** God does not patch the old; He births the new. The Spirit rewires the emotional and energetic circuits of the heart, allowing divine frequencies—faith, love, and joy—to flow without obstruction.

When this occurs, believers begin to radiate the energy of God's glory. Just as science measures the heart's electromagnetic field extending several feet beyond the body, the Spirit reveals that the glory of God can emanate from a purified heart—touching lives, healing atmospheres, and drawing others to Christ. This is not mysticism; it is **Kingdom physics**. The unseen laws of heaven govern both creation and the believer's inner world.

In this alignment, **Spirit commands, heart believes, mind agrees, and body obeys**. That is dominion—the complete synchronization of human nature with divine purpose.

End-of-Chapter Framework

Self-Reflection Questions

1. What beliefs currently rule the throne of my heart?
2. Do my thoughts and emotions reflect the authority of God or the authority of fear?
3. In what ways can I invite the Holy Spirit to govern my heart's decisions before my mind reacts?

Devotional Insight (Redirected, Readjusted, Set Aright, Increased in Holiness)

The Spirit redirects your attention from outward control to inward surrender. As your heart is readjusted to truth, your mind is set aright, and holiness increases through every cell of your being. The dominion of the heart is the dominion of peace.

Affirmation of Faith

"My heart is the dwelling place of divine wisdom.

God's Spirit governs my thoughts, renews my mind, and strengthens my body.

I live in harmony with His glory."

Prayer of Activation

Father, I yield my heart completely to You.

Cleanse every chamber where fear, pride, or sorrow has sat in authority.

Let Your Spirit dwell and reign within me.

Teach my heart to think with Your wisdom, to feel with Your compassion, and to command my body with divine strength.

In the name of Jesus, Amen.

Scripture Anchors

- *Proverbs 23:7* — "As a man thinketh in his heart, so is he."
- *Ezekiel 36:26* — "A new heart also will I give you, and a new spirit will I put within you."

Key Takeaways

- The heart is both a spiritual and biological center of intelligence.
- True transformation begins when the heart governs the mind and body under God's rule.
- Divine alignment restores emotional health, mental clarity, and physical vitality.

Call to Action

Take time today to listen to your heart in the presence of God.

Write down what He reveals and speak His truth aloud.

Each confession retrains the heart's brain to believe in alignment with divine authority.

CHAPTER TWO

God's View: Man Looks Outward, God Looks Within

"For the Lord does not see as man sees; for man looks at the outward appearance, but the Lord looks at the heart." — 1 Samuel 16:7 (AMP)

Part A — Revelation and Illumination

When God sent Samuel to anoint a new king for Israel, the prophet looked upon Eliab—strong, handsome, and seemingly qualified. But God stopped him and said, *"Do not consider his appearance or his height, for I have rejected him. The Lord looks at the heart."*

That single statement unveiled the eternal truth that governs all of heaven's decisions: **God measures from the inside out.**

Human beings tend to live from the outside in. We observe, compare, judge, and interpret based on what we can see. We assess success by performance, value by possessions, and worth by appearance. Yet none of these indicators reveal the true state of a person's being.

Heaven's measurement is different. **The heart is God's primary instrument of evaluation**—the chamber where motives are weighed, intentions purified, and truth revealed. Outward acts may deceive the eye, but the heart tells the truth of who we really are.

Your heart is the place where divine light searches out hidden rooms. The Spirit of God moves through its corridors like a lamp, exposing what is false and igniting what is pure. Proverbs 20:27 declares, *"The spirit of man is the lamp of the Lord, searching all the innermost parts of his being."*

To walk in the Kingdom is to allow this divine searchlight to govern you daily. It is not condemnation; it is correction through compassion. The Lord examines the heart not to shame you but to shape you—to align your inner atmosphere with His glory.

When we live for outward validation, we forfeit inward transformation. The approval of people can never sustain the peace of God. True power begins where human applause ends—inside the surrendered heart that whispers, "Lord, reign within me."

Part B — Kingdom Perspective and Inner Alignment

God's view is not limited by circumstance or behavior. He sees what is being *formed* within you. While the world reacts to results, God responds to roots.

If the root is holy, the fruit will be righteous. If the heart is yielded, the outcome will bear eternal weight.

The mind records memories, but the heart preserves motives. Every choice begins as a seed within the unseen soil of the heart. Jesus said, *"A good man out of the good treasure of his heart brings forth good things."* (Matthew 12:35) This means that our lives are simply outward reflections of inward storage.

The heart is the altar of agreement. It agrees either with heaven or with the flesh. When your heart aligns with the Spirit of God, divine order governs your thoughts, emotions, and body. But when the heart agrees with fear, pride, or resentment, it releases frequencies that distort perception and block revelation.

That is why the Father continually calls His people to a deeper posture of surrender. He is not seeking perfection; He is seeking **purity**—a heart that welcomes His gaze and invites His rule. A pure heart is a transparent one: nothing hidden, nothing hardened. Such a heart becomes a channel through which the glory of God flows freely, illuminating every part of the soul.

Kingdom dominion begins not with external conquest but with **internal governance**. When the heart is right, the mind becomes peaceful; when the heart is peaceful, the body follows with strength. This is the alignment of Spirit, Mind, and Body that manifests divine wholeness.

You are never more powerful than when your inner life reflects the heart of God. For from the heart flow "the issues of life" (Proverbs 4:23)—not just emotions, but direction, health, discernment, and authority.

To live from the inside out is to embody the very nature of the Kingdom—where unseen truth governs visible reality.

End-of-Chapter Framework

Self-Reflection Questions

1. What areas of my life still seek human approval rather than God's validation?
2. When was the last time I invited God to search the rooms of my heart without resistance?
3. How does knowing that God values the unseen parts of me change my view of success and holiness?

Devotional Insight (Redirected, Readjusted, Set Aright, Increased in Holiness)

The Spirit redirects your focus from performance to purity.

He readjusts your priorities to reflect heaven's values, not earthly praise.

He sets aright every motive, transforming hidden insecurity into holy intimacy.

Holiness increases when the heart welcomes the eyes of the Lord without fear.

Affirmation of Faith

"My worth is measured by God's gaze, not man's glance.

My heart is His dwelling, my motives His mirror.

The light of Christ rules within me, guiding my spirit, renewing my mind, and strengthening my body."

Prayer of Renewal

Father, search me and know my heart.

Expose every corner where pride, fear, or self-reliance has hidden.

Wash me with Your truth and renew a right spirit within me.

Let Your glory dwell in my inward parts until my outer life reflects Your image.

In Jesus' name, Amen.

Scripture Anchors

- *1 Samuel 16:7* — "Man looks at the outward appearance, but the Lord looks at the heart."
- *Psalm 51:6* — "Behold, You desire truth in the inward parts, and in the hidden part You make me to know wisdom."

Key Takeaways

- God measures character from the inside out.
- The heart is the seat of motive and the foundation of divine perception.
- Outward transformation begins with inward surrender.
- Wholeness flows when Spirit, Mind, and Body agree under divine governance.

Call to Action

Find a quiet space and invite the Holy Spirit to shine His light within your heart.

Write down what He reveals—truths, corrections, or affirmations of love.

Each revelation becomes a stone in the altar of transformation, where God's view becomes your own.

CHAPTER THREE

The Heart as a House of Authority

"Keep and guard your heart with all vigilance and above all that you guard, for out of it flow the springs of life." — Proverbs 4:23 (AMP)

Part A — Revelation and Definition

The heart is more than emotion—it is **a living government within the human spirit**. It is the seat of decision, the throne of belief, and the chamber where divine and human will meet. In Hebrew, the word translated *heart* is *levah* (לבב), composed of two ancient symbols: **Lamed**, the shepherd's staff of authority, and **Beth**, the house or dwelling. Together they declare a profound mystery—**the heart is the "house of authority."**

Within this sacred house, every thought, emotion, and conviction finds its origin. It is where faith is conceived, worship is born, and obedience begins. God designed the heart to rule the rest of our being. The brain may analyze, but the heart decides. The body may react, but the heart directs.

When Scripture says, *"Guard your heart with all diligence,"* it is not a suggestion—it is a command to protect the very government of your life. The heart is the spiritual embassy of heaven within you. Whatever gains entry there will rule your world. If peace reigns in the heart, it will be reflected in your thoughts, tone, and body. But if fear, bitterness, or unbelief take the throne, chaos will manifest outwardly.

The heart carries the right of **jurisdiction**—the power to issue decrees that the mind and body must obey. Science confirms this truth: the heart sends more signals to the brain than the brain sends to the heart. God's design ensures that spiritual governance begins from the inside out, not from the intellect downward.

Part B — Kingdom Insight and Application

Every believer is called to establish God's Kingdom within before manifesting it without. Jesus said, *"The Kingdom of God is within you."* (Luke 17:21) That inner Kingdom is administered from the heart. It is there that you host the King Himself.

When the heart is divided, your authority is diminished. James 1:8 warns, *"A double-minded man is unstable in all his ways."* The word *mind* here points back to the heart's thoughts—the inner seat of belief. To live with Kingdom stability, your heart must be unified under the Lordship of Christ.

Think of the heart as the governor's seat of a vast territory—your spirit, mind, and body. The spirit provides divine law, the mind records it, but the heart enforces it. It is the executive branch of your being. When the heart decrees faith, the mind aligns its thoughts, and the body follows in obedience. This is why miracles occur not when we think we believe, but when our **heart truly believes**.

Romans 10:10 declares, *"For with the heart one believes unto righteousness, and with the mouth confession is made unto salvation."* Belief is a function of the heart's authority. What your heart believes determines what your life will produce.

To live in the heart's dominion is to recognize that your internal world is a Kingdom in miniature. The Spirit of God dwells there as King. The conscience acts as judge, discerning between truth and deception. The will serves as the executor of law. The emotions are messengers, reporting to the throne. And the mind is the scribe, recording the decrees.

When this inner government is surrendered to God, heaven's order is established within, and your outer world begins to mirror the peace and power of divine rule.

But when this house of authority is neglected—when unclean influences are allowed entry—spiritual rebellion begins. Anxiety, confusion, and physical illness can often trace their roots to a dethroned heart. That is why continual consecration is vital. As priests of our own temple, we must guard the sanctuary daily, ensuring that nothing contrary to the Spirit's reign is allowed to linger.

Consecration is not confinement; it is freedom through alignment. When God's authority reigns within, every other power bows. The heart becomes a stronghold of light, radiating strength to the mind and vitality to the body.

End-of-Chapter Framework

Self-Reflection Questions

1. What influences have I allowed to enter the house of my heart without spiritual permission?
2. Which emotions or thoughts currently sit on the throne that belongs to God alone?
3. How can I strengthen the walls of my heart through worship, prayer, and the Word?

Devotional Insight (Redirected, Readjusted, Set Aright, Increased in Holiness)

The Spirit redirects your understanding of authority from the external to the internal.

He readjusts your vision, teaching you that rulership begins in surrender.

He sets aright the balance of power between your heart, mind, and body.

And as holiness increases, your inner house becomes a reflection of God's dwelling place.

Affirmation of Faith

"My heart is God's house of authority.

His Spirit rules within me with wisdom and peace.

My thoughts submit to His truth, and my body obeys His command.

I live under divine government and walk in holy order."

Prayer of Consecration

Father, I welcome Your presence into the chambers of my heart.

Cleanse my inner house from every thought or emotion that resists Your authority.

Establish Your throne within me and govern every decision through Your Spirit.

May my mind serve Your wisdom and my body manifest Your strength.

In Jesus' name, Amen.

Scripture Anchors

- *Proverbs 4:23* — "Keep and guard your heart with all vigilance, for out of it flow the springs of life."
- *Romans 10:10* — "For with the heart one believes unto righteousness."

Key Takeaways

- The heart is the spiritual government of the human being.
- Authority flows from the heart to the mind and body.
- The heart's purity determines the stability of your entire life.
- Surrendering the heart's throne to God restores divine order.

Call to Action

Set aside intentional moments this week to "inspect your house."

Ask the Holy Spirit to reveal what occupies your heart's throne.

Remove every intruder—fear, doubt, offense—and enthrone God once again through worship and obedience.

When the King reigns within, peace and dominion reign without.

CHAPTER FOUR

The Hebraic Meaning of *Levah*: A Dwelling for Divine Rule

"I will give them one heart and one way, that they may fear Me forever, for the good of them and of their children after them." — Jeremiah 32:39 (AMP)

Part A — Revelation and Definition

Every language carries spiritual weight, but Hebrew is unlike any other. It is the original language of divine revelation—where each letter is not only a sound, but a symbol, a number, and a revelation of God's intent.

When we examine the Hebrew word for *heart*, **Levah** (לבב), its letters reveal the architecture of divine order built into humanity.

- **Lamed (ל)** – a shepherd's staff or rod of authority; it signifies teaching, guidance, and rulership.
- **Beth (ב)** – a house or dwelling, representing the inner sanctuary, the habitation of God's presence.

Together, **Levah** means *"the house of authority"*—a place where rulership is exercised and divine order flows.

This is no poetic coincidence. From the moment God breathed life into Adam, He placed within the human heart the capacity to host His Spirit and govern creation under His command. The heart was formed as a **temple of divine instruction**—the meeting point between heaven and humanity.

When man fell, that temple became desecrated. The staff of authority (Lamed) remained, but the house (Beth) was filled with another voice. Sin enthroned self where God once sat. Yet God's redemptive plan was never to abandon the house but to restore its rightful ruler. That restoration is accomplished through the new birth and continual sanctification of the heart.

The divine intention has always been that **the heart of man would be the dwelling of God**, not a battlefield of confusion.

Part B — Spiritual Blueprint and Kingdom Application

When the Spirit of God takes residence within the heart, the letters of *Levah* are reanimated. The shepherd's staff (authority) and the house (dwelling) become one in purpose. The result is divine rulership expressed through human surrender.

Jesus declared in John 14:23, *"If anyone loves Me, he will keep My word; and My Father will love him, and We will come to him and make Our home with him."*

This home is the heart—the *Beth* of your being. It is here that God sets His throne, and from this sanctuary His Word is written, not on stone tablets but on living hearts (2 Corinthians 3:3).

When we understand the Hebraic structure of the heart, we see why every decision we make flows from this sacred space. The heart is not an emotional chamber; it is a governmental one. It decides which kingdom—light or darkness—will reign in our inner house.

Lamed (authority) must always be held by God's hand. When our authority is self-driven, it leads to pride and disorder. But when we surrender that staff to the Good Shepherd, our leadership becomes service, our rulership becomes humility, and our power becomes peace.

Beth (house) must always remain consecrated. A house divided cannot stand. The heart cannot simultaneously host God's glory and harbor unrepentant sin. Just as the priests of old purified the temple daily, we must continually cleanse the inner dwelling with repentance, worship, and the washing of the Word.

The Kingdom principle is this: **The measure of divine authority we walk in outwardly depends on the measure of divine presence we host inwardly.**

The word *Levah* therefore becomes not just a linguistic term but a prophetic design—a call to reestablish God's dominion in the heart so that spirit, mind, and body may function as one in His glory.

The shepherd's staff of authority and the house of habitation are meant to be inseparable. One rules; the other hosts. One commands; the other contains. Together, they create a sanctuary of divine government—a living temple from which the Kingdom of God is revealed through you.

End-of-Chapter Framework

Self-Reflection Questions

1. Who currently holds the staff of authority in my heart—God's Spirit or my self-will?
2. Is my inner house cleansed, or have I allowed distractions and doubts to dwell there?
3. What steps can I take daily to reestablish God's throne in the dwelling place of my heart?

Devotional Insight (Redirected, Readjusted, Set Aright, Increased in Holiness)

The Spirit redirects your understanding of the heart as a symbol to the heart as a structure.

He readjusts your inner posture, teaching you to yield authority back to its rightful Owner.

He sets aright the spiritual blueprint within you, connecting divine rulership with human obedience.

As holiness increases, your heart becomes the true *Beth*—the holy dwelling of the Most High.

Affirmation of Faith

"My heart is God's dwelling.

His authority leads me like a shepherd's staff.

My inner house is holy, my emotions sanctified, my thoughts aligned.

The Lord reigns within me, and His peace governs my soul."

Prayer of Dedication

Heavenly Father,

I offer You the house of my heart.

Cleanse its walls, repair its altars, and restore Your throne within.

Take hold of the staff of authority that I once misused, and rule over every area of my life.

Let my heart become Your Beth—Your holy habitation of wisdom, peace, and glory.

In Jesus' name, Amen.

Scripture Anchors

- *Jeremiah 32:39* — "I will give them one heart and one way, that they may fear Me forever."
- *John 14:23* — "We will come to him and make Our home with him."

Key Takeaways

- The Hebrew word *Levah* reveals the heart as the "house of authority."

- Divine rule flows from the union of authority (*Lamed*) and habitation (*Beth*).
- True Kingdom leadership begins within the cleansed heart.
- Hosting God's presence restores dominion and releases peace throughout the whole being.

Call to Action

Meditate today on the letters of *Levah*—Lamed and Beth.

Visualize handing the staff of your heart back to the Shepherd and preparing the house for His glory.

As you worship, declare aloud: "Lord, my heart is Your home."

Every act of surrender rebuilds the sanctuary of your inner life, brick by brick, until it reflects heaven on earth.

CHAPTER FIVE

The Glory Field: Energy, Presence, and Spiritual Emission

"Arise, shine, for your light has come, and the glory of the Lord has risen upon you." — Isaiah 60:1 (AMP)

Part A — Revelation and Definition

There is a light that cannot be seen with the human eye but can be felt in the soul. It is the radiance that emanates from a heart surrendered to God—the **glory field**.

In scientific terms, this field might be described as an **electromagnetic energy** emitted by the heart, measurable up to six feet beyond the body. But in the Kingdom, this field represents the **manifestation of divine presence** flowing from within a believer who lives in spiritual alignment.

The human heart produces an electromagnetic field 5,000 times stronger than that of the brain and emits a frequency that synchronizes with every cell in the body. When the heart is filled with peace, gratitude, and faith, this field becomes coherent, releasing harmony into the physical, emotional, and even atmospheric environment around you.

Yet, science is only describing what the Spirit has revealed for millennia. When God dwells within the human heart, His glory radiates outward, touching everything it encounters. This divine radiation is not merely symbolic—it is **spiritual energy in motion**. The same power that hovered over the waters in Genesis now flows from within those who are filled with His Spirit.

The heart, then, is more than an organ; it is a **portal of divine emission**. When purified and governed by love, it becomes a transmitter of heaven's frequency—a living lamp broadcasting the glory of God to the world.

When Jesus walked the earth, people could sense His presence before He spoke. The woman with the issue of blood said, *"If I can but touch the hem of His garment, I shall be made whole."* (Mark 5:28) She was not merely touching fabric—she was touching the radiant field of divine virtue that flowed from His heart. Scripture says, *"Power went out from Him."* That power was the **glory field** of a perfect, sinless heart in full union with the Spirit.

Part B — The Spiritual Dynamics of Emission

The **glory field** is the natural byproduct of inner sanctification. When your heart becomes unified with God's Spirit, your entire being becomes a vessel of transmission. This is why Paul wrote, *"We have this treasure in earthen vessels, that the excellency of the power may be of God, and not of us."* (2 Corinthians 4:7)

Every thought and emotion you release carries a frequency. Fear emits distortion; faith emits order. Bitterness radiates heaviness; gratitude radiates peace.

The heart's field, whether sanctified or polluted, affects everything within its range. When the believer abides in holiness and love, that field becomes a **sphere of glory**—a zone of healing, peace, and divine magnetism.

This is what Jesus referred to when He said, *"You are the light of the world."* (Matthew 5:14) Light here represents energy, revelation, and spiritual influence. The light of the Kingdom does not shine merely from words but from **presence**—from the life-force of one who hosts God within.

When your heart is aligned with heaven, the Spirit's frequency resonates through your being. People will feel the peace before you speak it, sense the love before you express it, and witness the power before you display it. You become a living evidence of Emmanuel—*God with us.*

The heart's electromagnetic field mirrors the **spiritual field of glory** described in Scripture. Moses' face shone after dwelling in the presence of God because his heart had absorbed divine radiance. Stephen's face appeared as that of an angel while he was being persecuted. These were not metaphors—they were manifestations of the **glory field** overflowing from within.

This radiance is not reserved for prophets or apostles alone. Every believer, when sanctified and filled with the Holy Spirit, carries this same potential. The heart's field expands with worship, obedience, and love. The more yielded you are, the greater the emission of glory around you.

Just as a lamp must be connected to its source to shine, so your heart must remain plugged into God's presence to release His energy. Sin and fear dim the light; faith and purity amplify it.

You were never meant to live dimmed—you were created to *glow with the glory of God.*

End-of-Chapter Framework

Self-Reflection Questions

1. What kind of energy do I radiate into my surroundings—peace or pressure, faith or fear?
2. How often do I intentionally connect my heart with God's presence to recharge my spiritual field?
3. In what ways can I become a visible reflection of invisible glory in my home, work, and ministry?

Devotional Insight (Redirected, Readjusted, Set Aright, Increased in Holiness)

The Spirit redirects your awareness from your outer influence to your inner condition.

He readjusts your perception, revealing that true power flows not from effort but from presence.

He sets aright your understanding that you are both the vessel and the transmitter of God's light.

As holiness increases, your energy field becomes radiant with divine coherence—the rhythm of heaven.

Affirmation of Faith

"The glory of God flows from my heart like living light.

I am a vessel of divine energy and a carrier of His peace.

My presence transforms atmospheres because His presence abides in me.

I radiate healing, joy, and life wherever I go."

Prayer of Activation

Father, fill my heart with Your glory until my entire being reflects Your light.

Cleanse my inner field of every shadow and teach me to emit Your peace.

Let Your power flow through me to heal, restore, and awaken others to Your love.

May my life radiate Your presence like a beacon in the darkness.

In Jesus' name, Amen.

Scripture Anchors

- *Isaiah 60:1* — "Arise, shine, for your light has come, and the glory of the Lord has risen upon you."
- *2 Corinthians 4:7* — "We have this treasure in earthen vessels, that the excellency of the power may be of God."

Key Takeaways

- The heart emits both physical and spiritual energy measurable as a field of influence.
- The **glory field** represents the presence and power of God radiating through a sanctified heart.

- Alignment with God increases coherence, creating harmony in body, mind, and environment.
- Every believer is a living transmitter of divine glory.

Call to Action

Spend intentional time in silence and worship today.

Visualize the light of God's Spirit filling your heart and expanding outward six feet or more, covering every space around you with peace and power.

Declare aloud: "The glory of the Lord rises upon me."

Walk through your day conscious of that field—every step you take releases His presence into the world

CHAPTER SIX

The Heart That Rules the Mind

"And the peace of God, which transcends all understanding, shall guard your hearts and your minds in Christ Jesus." — Philippians 4:7 (AMP)

Part A — Revelation and Definition

For many, the mind appears to be the ruler—the domain where logic, decisions, and understanding take form. Yet the Word of God reveals a deeper truth: the mind is the **servant**, not the master. The **heart** is the true seat of government.

The **heart rules the mind** because belief always precedes thought. The heart is the throne where conviction resides; the mind is the court that interprets and executes its decrees. The brain receives its direction from the emotional and spiritual command center of the heart.

Science confirms what Scripture has declared: the heart sends more messages to the brain than the brain sends to the heart. Neurological studies show that the heart influences perception, cognition, and emotional balance. But the Kingdom goes even further—it teaches that the heart's spiritual condition governs how the mind interprets reality.

When the heart is fearful, the mind becomes anxious.

When the heart is proud, the mind becomes critical.

When the heart is bitter, the mind becomes confused.

But when the heart is filled with peace, the mind becomes clear; when the heart is full of love, the mind becomes sound; and when the heart is surrendered to God, the mind becomes renewed.

Romans 12:2 says, *"Be transformed by the renewing of your mind."* That transformation begins not in the brain but in the **heart**—for it is the heart that determines what the mind will focus on and how it will interpret truth.

A heart ruled by God produces a mind ruled by peace.

Part B — Kingdom Insight and Mental Renewal

The human mind is powerful, but without a sanctified heart, it becomes a wandering instrument—brilliant yet directionless. The heart provides moral and spiritual boundaries for thought. It is the compass that keeps intellect aligned with divine purpose.

When the Spirit reigns in your heart, your mind comes under the influence of heavenly peace. The Apostle Paul writes that God's peace "shall garrison and mount guard over your hearts and minds." (Philippians 4:7) The image is military—peace acts as a soldier guarding both the command center (the heart) and the observatory (the mind).

This means that the battles of mental torment, overthinking, anxiety, and confusion are not won through logic but through **alignment**. The mind finds rest when the heart is surrendered. Mental healing flows not from control but from trust—trust that God governs from within.

When we allow the Spirit to establish dominion in the heart, the mind begins to reflect heaven's clarity. This is what Jesus demonstrated in His earthly walk. His peace was unshakeable because His heart was fully yielded to the Father's will. Every thought He spoke carried Kingdom authority because His mind operated under the command of a sanctified heart.

You were designed to think from your heart. That is why the Word says, *"Let the peace of God rule in your hearts."* (Colossians 3:15) The word *rule* in Greek means "to act as an umpire"—to make the final decision. When peace is enthroned in the heart, it calls every thought into divine order.

Every time you choose forgiveness over anger, you shift the authority from the carnal mind to the spiritual heart. Every time you meditate on the Word, you are retraining your mind to obey the Spirit's voice that speaks within your heart.

This is the pathway to mental healing and spiritual maturity: the heart governs, the mind submits, and the body follows.

When your heart is right with God, your mind becomes a mirror of His wisdom.

End-of-Chapter Framework

Self-Reflection Questions

1. Who currently rules the decisions of my mind—my emotions, my fears, or the Spirit of God?
2. What thoughts arise most often, and what do they reveal about the condition of my heart?
3. How can I daily realign my mind to serve the peace that rules my heart?

Devotional Insight (Redirected, Readjusted, Set Aright, Increased in Holiness)

The Spirit redirects your reliance from intellect to intimacy.

He readjusts your focus from controlling thoughts to surrendering the heart.

He sets aright the divine hierarchy: spirit above heart, heart above mind.

As holiness increases, the mind becomes still, and the peace of God flows like a river through every thought.

Affirmation of Faith

"My heart is the throne of God's peace.

My mind serves the wisdom of the Spirit.

Every thought is brought under obedience to Christ.

I think with clarity, I feel with compassion, and I live with confidence in His rule."

Prayer of Renewal

Father, I yield the government of my heart to You.

Let Your peace be enthroned within me and Your wisdom rule over my thoughts.

Where confusion once lived, plant understanding.

Where fear once whispered, speak faith.

Renew my mind as my heart abides in Your presence.

In Jesus' name, Amen.

Scripture Anchors

- *Philippians 4:7* — "The peace of God shall guard your hearts and minds in Christ Jesus."
- *Romans 12:2* — "Be transformed by the renewing of your mind."

Key Takeaways

- The mind is directed by the heart's spiritual condition.
- Mental peace flows from a heart ruled by divine authority.
- The Spirit governs the heart, and the heart governs thought.
- True transformation begins inwardly, not intellectually.

Call to Action

Pause several times today and ask: *What is ruling my thoughts right now?*

If anxiety or fear is present, return to the heart.

Place your hand over your chest, breathe deeply, and declare:

"Peace of God, rule in my heart. Mind of Christ, govern my thoughts."

Repeat until calm arises—this is the alignment of the heart's dominion restoring order to your mind.

CHAPTER SEVEN

Guarding the Gate of Your Inner House

"Above all else, guard your heart, for everything you do flows from it." — *Proverbs 4:23 (NIV)*

Part A — Revelation and Definition

Every Kingdom has gates. Every dwelling has doors. Every heart has entry points. The question is not whether your heart has gates—it does—but *who* has access to them.

The **heart** is a sacred house, the dwelling of God's Spirit, the seat of will, emotion, and faith. Its gates are the **pathways of influence**—what we see, hear, feel, meditate on, and imagine. These gateways determine what enters to shape our beliefs and emotions, and ultimately, our lives.

When the Word of God commands, *"Guard your heart,"* it is giving us the divine protocol for Kingdom security. Guarding is not passive; it is an act of **spiritual watchfulness**—the continual discernment of what is being allowed into the house of authority.

What the enemy cannot conquer, he tries to corrupt. His strategy has always been infiltration. He seeks to plant distortion through unguarded gates: a bitter word that takes root, a fearful thought that becomes belief, an image that stirs temptation. If the gates remain open without discernment, the house becomes vulnerable.

Guarding the heart means setting divine boundaries that protect the flow of life within. The heart is not meant to be sealed from love, but it must be **secured from pollution.**

Imagine your heart as a royal city. The Spirit of God dwells in the inner chamber; the mind acts as the gatekeeper; the senses form the outer walls. When the gates are unguarded, unholy influences trespass the soul. But when the Spirit rules at the gates, everything entering or leaving must align with truth, purity, and peace.

To "guard" is to **watch with intention**—to become aware of what is shaping your inner world.

Part B — Kingdom Insight and Application

The Hebrew word for *guard* in Proverbs 4:23 is *natsar*, which means *to preserve, to protect, to maintain with fidelity*. It is the same word used for keeping a vineyard. A wise gardener doesn't simply plant seed and walk away; they inspect, prune, and protect it daily. So must you do with your heart.

Guarding begins with awareness:

- **What you feed your mind** becomes the material of your meditation.
- **What you dwell upon emotionally** becomes the climate of your soul.
- **What you agree with spiritually** becomes the law of your heart.

Therefore, guarding requires spiritual discipline and emotional maturity. You must become both **priest and watchman** of your own heart—ministering truth within while keeping the walls intact against intrusion.

The gate of **sight** must be sanctified: not everything seen is meant to be stored.

The gate of **hearing** must be filtered: not every voice deserves access to your inner conversation.

The gate of **thought** must be renewed: not every idea should be entertained.

The Apostle Paul gives the blueprint for guarding the mind and heart:

"Whatever is true, whatever is honorable, whatever is right, whatever is pure, whatever is lovely, whatever is admirable—if there is any excellence or anything worthy of praise—think on these things." (Philippians 4:8)

This passage is not merely about positivity—it's about *protection*. Each word defines the materials allowed through your gate. When these become the standard of entry, the house remains filled with light.

Guarding your heart is not about fear of contamination but about preservation of glory. The more you value what God has entrusted to you, the more intentionally you will protect it.

To live in continual peace and authority, you must adopt the mindset of a gatekeeper: *What I permit determines what I produce.*

Every guarded moment fortifies your dominion.

End-of-Chapter Framework

Self-Reflection Questions

1. What have I allowed through my heart's gates that has weakened my peace or clarity?
2. Which gate—sight, hearing, emotion, thought, or memory—needs reinforcement today?
3. How can I invite the Holy Spirit to stand watch over the entrances of my inner house?

Devotional Insight (Redirected, Readjusted, Set Aright, Increased in Holiness)

The Spirit redirects your focus from outward control to inward guardianship.

He readjusts your gates, restoring spiritual discipline and sensitivity.

He sets aright your boundaries, teaching you to preserve the flow of divine life.

As holiness increases, you become both the temple and its watchman, secure in His peace.

Affirmation of Faith

"My heart is a sacred house of God's presence.

The Holy Spirit guards its gates and governs its flow.

No fear, impurity, or deception has access to my inner life.

I live in divine security, peace, and purity."

Prayer of Guarding

Father, You are the Keeper of my soul and the Guardian of my heart.

Teach me to recognize every doorway that allows influence.

Close what is unclean; open what is pure.

Set Your angels at my gates and Your Spirit as my shield.

Let my heart remain a fortress of truth and a dwelling of peace.

In Jesus' name, Amen.

Scripture Anchors

- *Proverbs 4:23* — "Above all else, guard your heart, for everything you do flows from it."
- *Philippians 4:8* — "Think on these things."

Key Takeaways

- Guarding the heart means managing access to your inner life.
- Every gate (sight, hearing, thought, emotion) must be sanctified.
- The Holy Spirit is both protector and peacekeeper within.
- Guarding the heart preserves divine authority and maintains Kingdom order.

Call to Action

Take inventory of your inner gates today.

Ask: *What am I allowing to enter through my eyes, ears, emotions, and thoughts?*

Then make adjustments—remove what pollutes, invite what purifies.

Spend five minutes in stillness declaring:

"My heart is guarded by God; my gates are secure in His peace."

Let that confession become your daily watchword.

CHAPTER EIGHT

When Authority Is Surrendered: How the Enemy Fills the Heart

"Then Satan entered into Judas called Iscariot, who was of the number of the twelve." — Luke 22:3 (AMP)

Part A — Revelation and Warning

The enemy has no creative power of his own; he can only **occupy what is surrendered**. He cannot create a heart, but he can inhabit one that abdicates its divine authority.

When Judas betrayed Jesus, Scripture says, *"Then Satan entered into him."* The word *entered* here means *to take possession through open access*. Judas did not lose authority overnight—it was **surrendered gradually**, through greed, resentment, and disobedience. Each compromise was a key handed over to the adversary until finally, the house was occupied by another spirit.

The same principle applies to all who live without spiritual vigilance. Every heart is a house of authority (Levah). Whoever sits on its throne directs the life. If God reigns, peace and light flow; if sin reigns, confusion and darkness spread. The enemy's first goal is not to destroy the body but to **displace divine rule** in the heart.

How does this happen? Not through sudden rebellion, but through subtle deception:

- A justified offense that becomes bitterness.
- A tolerated fear that becomes unbelief.
- A neglected prayer life that becomes spiritual apathy.

Every unguarded moment creates entry points. The heart that was once a dwelling of worship can become a storage room for wounds, resentments, and lies. Once authority is surrendered, influence shifts. The mind becomes tormented, the emotions unstable, and the body weary.

The heart cannot remain unoccupied; it must be filled by something. When it is not filled with the Spirit, it becomes open to other spirits.

Part B — Kingdom Revelation and Restoration

When authority is surrendered, the goal of restoration is not self-repair—it is **reestablishing divine government**. Repentance is the act of evicting foreign tenants and inviting the rightful King back to His throne.

David understood this principle when he cried, *"Create in me a clean heart, O God, and renew a right spirit within me."* (Psalm 51:10) He didn't ask for a stronger will or a better strategy; he asked for **a clean heart**—because he knew the seat of authority determines the flow of life.

In Kingdom terms, restoration means **reclaiming jurisdiction**. The Spirit of God does not wrestle for control; He reigns where He is welcomed. As soon as the heart yields, heaven reenters. Peace replaces chaos, discernment replaces confusion, and the heart's throne is reestablished under divine dominion.

Surrendered authority can always be recovered through repentance. The enemy's occupation is never permanent when the heart returns to its Maker.

God's mercy is not just forgiveness—it is *reinstallation of divine order.* The moment you acknowledge, "Lord, I've let other voices rule my heart," the Spirit begins the process of cleansing and restoration. The glory returns, the light expands, and the gates are resealed.

The enemy's greatest fear is a believer who knows how to reclaim territory. You were not designed to live invaded; you were designed to **rule from within**.

When divine authority is restored, the same heart that once housed fear becomes a fortress of faith. The same emotions that once carried pain become rivers of peace.

You are never too far gone to be restored—the King still desires His throne.

End-of-Chapter Framework

Self-Reflection Questions

1. Have I unconsciously surrendered areas of my heart's authority through compromise, fear, or offense?
2. What patterns or emotions have gained control where God once reigned?
3. How can I intentionally invite the Holy Spirit to reclaim full dominion in my heart today?

Devotional Insight (Redirected, Readjusted, Set Aright, Increased in Holiness)

The Spirit redirects your awareness from condemnation to conviction.

He readjusts your view of repentance—from shame to restoration.

He sets aright your inner throne, replacing self-rule with divine governance.

As holiness increases, your heart becomes unshakable, and the enemy's influence is silenced.

Affirmation of Faith

"My heart is the throne of God's rule.

No other voice or power holds authority within me.

Through repentance, I reclaim my territory.

The Spirit reigns in me; peace governs my mind; righteousness restores my soul."

Prayer of Restoration

Father, I come before You with an open heart.

If I have surrendered any part of my inner house to fear, pride, or deception, I renounce it now.

Cleanse me from hidden faults and restore Your throne within me.

Evict every intruder that has spoken lies into my soul.

Reign again, O King of Glory, in every chamber of my being.

Let Your Spirit fill me until nothing unholy remains.

In Jesus' name, Amen.

Scripture Anchors

- *Luke 22:3* — "Then Satan entered into Judas."
- *Psalm 51:10* — "Create in me a clean heart, O God, and renew a right spirit within me."

Key Takeaways

- The enemy gains access only through surrendered authority.
- Compromise and neglect open gates for infiltration.
- Repentance reestablishes divine government in the heart.
- God's mercy restores what rebellion displaced.

Call to Action

Take time today to write a *"Declaration of Repossession."*

List every area where you've felt fear, anger, or compromise.

Beside each one, write: **"I reclaim this territory for the Kingdom of God."**

Pray aloud, inviting the Holy Spirit to fill every space once occupied by darkness.

As you do, visualize the throne of your heart being reestablished in light—firm, radiant, and secure.

CHAPTER NINE

The Language of the Heart: How God Speaks from Within

"My sheep hear My voice, and I know them, and they follow Me." — John 10:27 (AMP)

Part A — Revelation and Definition

The greatest mystery of spiritual communication is not that God speaks—it is *where* He speaks.

Most people search for God in the sky, in the storm, in the signs and wonders, yet Scripture repeatedly draws our attention inward: "The Kingdom of God is within you." (Luke 17:21)

The heart is the spiritual receiver of divine communication—the **inner chamber where heaven and earth meet**. It is in the heart that the whisper of God becomes audible to the soul.

When the Spirit of God speaks, He does not always use words. He speaks in impressions, peace, conviction, illumination, and love. These are the dialects of divine language that flow through the heart's spiritual intelligence.

The **language of the heart** is not heard by the ears but *felt by the soul*. It is recognized not by emotion but by resonance—when your spirit agrees with the truth being revealed.

In Hebrew thought, to "hear" God means more than sound; it means *to obey, to respond, to internalize.* The word *shema* means "to hear and to do." Thus, when Jesus said, *"He who has ears to hear, let him hear,"* He was not referring to physical hearing but to **spiritual receptivity**—the ability of the heart to discern and obey.

The voice of God is never distant; it is discerned through purity of heart. Sin and fear create static, but holiness and stillness create clarity. That is why Psalm 46:10 says, *"Be still and know that I am God."* Stillness is the atmosphere of revelation.

The Spirit speaks from within the believer through three main channels of the heart:

1. **Conviction** — correction and guidance for righteousness.
2. **Peace** — confirmation of divine alignment.
3. **Desire** — inspiration planted by God to lead toward purpose.

When these harmonize, you can trust that what you sense is not mere emotion but divine communication.

Part B — Kingdom Insight and Discernment

Learning the language of the heart requires both humility and practice. Just as a child learns the voice of a parent through intimacy, believers learn the voice of God through relationship, not religion.

God does not compete with noise; He speaks through *peace.*

He does not argue with doubt; He imparts *assurance.*

He does not command with fear; He draws with *love.*

The Spirit's voice always carries the fruit of His nature—love, joy, peace, patience, kindness, goodness, faithfulness, gentleness, and self-control (Galatians 5:22–23).

If what you sense brings panic, accusation, or confusion, it is not the voice of God.

If what you sense brings conviction but peace, direction but freedom, that is His language.

The heart communicates with layers of meaning beyond words. Sometimes you will "feel" truth before you can articulate it. Sometimes you will sense danger before evidence appears. Sometimes a verse, a phrase, or a thought will rise in your heart repeatedly—like a divine echo. These are all signals that the Spirit is speaking.

In this way, the **heart is heaven's interpreter**. The brain translates what the heart receives, but revelation originates from within the spirit-man, not the intellect.

When your heart is clean, the signal becomes clear.

When your heart is cluttered, the signal becomes distorted.

Discernment, therefore, is not merely a gift; it is the fruit of alignment. The more you align your heart with the Spirit, the easier it becomes to distinguish His voice from all others.

The Prophet Elijah discovered this truth in the cave. He expected God in the wind, the earthquake, and the fire—but the Lord was not there. Then came a still small voice. (1 Kings 19:11–12) That whisper was not external—it was internal, resonating in his spirit.

God's preferred communication system is not thunder—it is intimacy.

He speaks most clearly when your heart is most still.

The mature believer learns to interpret this language of resonance:

- The *peace* of God is the punctuation of His sentence.
- The *conviction* of God is the clarity of His command.
- The *joy* of God is the confirmation of His presence.

To live by this inner dialogue is to walk in continual fellowship with the Holy Spirit. You become fluent in the language of heaven.

End-of-Chapter Framework

Self-Reflection Questions

1. How do I currently discern the voice of God—through peace, conviction, or external confirmation?
2. Are there emotional noises or distractions clouding the stillness of my heart?
3. What practices help me remain sensitive to the inner language of the Spirit?

Devotional Insight (Redirected, Readjusted, Set Aright, Increased in Holiness)

The Spirit redirects your dependence from external validation to internal revelation.

He readjusts your frequency, tuning your heart to heaven's signal.

He sets aright your inner receiver, clearing interference caused by fear or sin.

As holiness increases, your heart becomes fluent in the language of God's love.

Affirmation of Faith

"My heart hears the voice of God.

His peace speaks louder than my fears.

His Spirit interprets every moment with divine wisdom.

I am guided by His inner whisper and governed by His love."

Prayer of Sensitivity

Father, open the ears of my heart to Your voice.

Teach me to discern Your whisper in the quiet moments.

Remove every noise of fear and confusion.

Let Your peace be the proof of Your presence.

May I live fluent in the language of heaven and quick to obey what You reveal.

In Jesus' name, Amen.

Scripture Anchors

- *John 10:27* — "My sheep hear My voice, and I know them, and they follow Me."
- *1 Kings 19:11-12* — "The Lord was not in the wind… but in a still small voice."

Key Takeaways

- The heart is God's communication center.
- The Spirit's language is peace, conviction, and love—not fear or confusion.
- Revelation flows through stillness, purity, and intimacy.

- Spiritual fluency grows as the heart aligns with the Spirit's frequency.

Call to Action

Spend 10 minutes today in silent stillness before God.

Quiet your thoughts and simply say, *"Speak, Lord, for Your servant is listening."*

Write down the first peaceful impression or scripture that rises in your heart.

Then meditate on it throughout the day.

As you practice this, your heart will grow fluent in recognizing the sound of divine love.

CHAPTER TEN

When the Heart and Spirit Agree: The Power of Inner Covenant

"Can two walk together, except they be agreed?" — Amos 3:3 (KJV)

Part A — Revelation and Definition

Every manifestation of God's power begins in **agreement**.

Agreement is the foundation of creation, the secret to Kingdom manifestation, and the bond that allows divine will to flow without resistance.

Before anything visible came into existence, **Spirit and Word were in perfect harmony.** God spoke, and the Spirit moved upon the waters. Creation was born through agreement between divine intention and divine power.

Within every believer, that same principle still governs transformation: **when the spirit and the heart agree, creation happens.**

The human **spirit** is the part of you that communes directly with God—it receives revelation, instruction, and divine impulses. The **heart** is the seat of belief and emotion—it receives revelation and translates it into conviction, action, and manifestation.

When the spirit perceives God's will but the heart resists in fear, there is conflict, and power cannot flow. But when your heart agrees with what your spirit knows, **the inner covenant is complete**—heaven and earth unite within you.

This is what Jesus meant when He said, *"If you believe in your heart…"* (Mark 11:23). Belief is the bridge between revelation and reality. Faith is not merely thinking God's Word is true—it is the inner harmony between what your spirit perceives and what your heart believes.

The enemy's main goal is to divide the two. He cannot destroy your spirit—it belongs to God—but he can distract your heart. A divided heart produces a divided life. The flow of divine power is interrupted when inner agreement is broken.

To walk in Kingdom dominion, your **heart and spirit must speak the same language.**

Part B — Kingdom Insight and Application

In the divine order of being, the spirit is the leader, the heart is the believer, and the mind is the interpreter. The spirit receives revelation; the heart embraces it as truth; the mind manifests it through words and actions.

When these three are in unity, divine energy flows unhindered. This unity is called the **inner covenant**—a binding agreement between your spirit and your heart under the authority of God's Spirit.

This covenant releases the creative and prophetic flow of the Kingdom.

When you speak from this place of inner agreement, your words carry divine weight.

When you pray from this place, heaven responds instantly, because there is no contradiction between your inner and outer being.

Jesus modeled this harmony perfectly. He said, *"The Son can do nothing by Himself; He does only what He sees the Father doing."* (John 5:19) His spirit was one with the Father, and His heart was in perfect agreement with that will. That unity produced miracles, authority, and peace.

Your life is meant to reflect the same. When your spirit and heart are aligned with the Father, every part of you becomes an instrument of Kingdom expression.

Here's the spiritual pattern:

1. **Revelation** — The Spirit reveals truth to your inner man.
2. **Agreement** — Your heart accepts it without fear or resistance.
3. **Activation** — Your faith releases it into manifestation.

Whenever you sense stagnation or confusion, check for *disagreement* within. Ask: *Has my heart believed what my spirit knows?* The spirit knows you are healed, chosen, powerful, and redeemed—but the heart may still carry residue of fear, guilt, or rejection. Healing occurs when the two reconcile under the truth of God's Word.

This is the mystery of **inner covenant**—heaven's contract written not on paper but on your heart. When that agreement is sealed, you walk not in striving but in flow. You do not *try* to manifest God's glory—you *become* the vessel through which it effortlessly moves.

When spirit and heart are one, you live in divine rhythm. The body follows, the mind obeys, and your words carry the vibration of heaven.

End-of-Chapter Framework

Self-Reflection Questions

1. Are my heart and spirit in full agreement, or do I sense conflict between belief and truth?
2. What truths has God spoken to my spirit that my heart still struggles to accept?
3. How can I cultivate deeper unity within so that God's will flows without resistance?

Devotional Insight (Redirected, Readjusted, Set Aright, Increased in Holiness)

The Spirit redirects your attention from outward warfare to inward agreement.

He readjusts your understanding that victory begins within, not without.

He sets aright your relationship between spirit and heart, teaching them to walk as one.

As holiness increases, your words align with heaven's tone, and your life becomes prophecy fulfilled.

Affirmation of Faith

"My spirit hears the voice of God.

My heart believes His truth without fear.

The two are one in purpose and power.

Through this inner covenant, I manifest His glory and walk in divine authority."

Prayer of Agreement

Father, I thank You for the covenant You have established within me.

Let my spirit and my heart walk in unity under Your rule.

Heal every fracture between what I know and what I believe.

Let truth become agreement, and agreement become manifestation.

From this day forward, may my inner being reflect perfect harmony with Your Spirit.

In Jesus' name, Amen.

Scripture Anchors

- *Amos 3:3* — "Can two walk together, except they be agreed?"
- *Mark 11:23* — "If you believe in your heart... it will be done."

Key Takeaways

- The spirit receives revelation; the heart believes it; the mind manifests it.
- Agreement between spirit and heart releases creative power.
- Division within produces delay; unity produces manifestation.
- The inner covenant is the gateway to Kingdom authority.

Call to Action

Spend time journaling what your spirit *knows* versus what your heart *feels*.

Write down any contradictions, and invite the Holy Spirit to reconcile them.

Pray, "Lord, make my heart agree with what my spirit already knows to be true."

As you practice this, you'll experience the peace, power, and creative flow that comes from inner covenant.

CHAPTER ELEVEN

The Frequency of Faith: How the Heart Transmits Belief into Reality

"Now faith is the substance of things hoped for, the evidence of things not seen."
— Hebrews 11:1 (AMP)

Part A — Revelation and Definition

Faith is more than a concept—it is an energy field, a spiritual vibration that resonates with the very nature of God. When Scripture says, *"The just shall live by faith,"* it is describing not merely a belief system but an entire frequency of existence—a way of being that transmits divine reality into the material world.

The **heart** is the transmitter of that frequency. When it believes, it broadcasts the vibration of conviction that calls unseen truth into physical form. This is why Jesus declared, *"If you believe in your heart and do not doubt... you will have whatever you say."* (Mark 11:23)

Belief originates in the heart because it is the bridge between the unseen (spirit) and the seen (matter). The heart speaks the language of energy—emotion, faith, passion, and love—and the universe, created by the Word of God, responds to that language.

In scientific understanding, every thought and emotion emits measurable frequencies that influence both the body and the environment. Spiritually, those frequencies are expressions of faith or fear—two opposite forces that shape reality.

Faith harmonizes with heaven.

Fear harmonizes with chaos.

The moment your heart believes, it begins transmitting an electromagnetic signal that aligns your environment with your conviction. That signal, when governed by the Holy Spirit, becomes a **Kingdom frequency**—a divine resonance that manifests God's will on earth.

Part B — Kingdom Insight and Spiritual Application

The **frequency of faith** is not achieved through effort—it is released through agreement. When the heart fully trusts what God has spoken, it enters divine rest. In that rest, energy becomes focused, intention becomes pure, and manifestation becomes inevitable.

Faith's vibration carries both **sound** and **substance**:

- **Sound**, because it echoes the Word of God already spoken.
- **Substance**, because it carries the blueprint of what is being created.

When God said, *"Let there be light,"* His Word did not create light through thought alone—it released frequency, vibration, and divine resonance that formed light out of invisible energy. In the same way, when you believe and speak under divine alignment, your heart releases a creative vibration that reshapes your world.

This is not metaphysical imagination—it is **spiritual law**. Hebrews 11:3 declares, *"By faith we understand that the worlds were framed by the Word of God."* The same creative force that framed the cosmos now flows through a believer's heart when aligned with heaven.

Every word spoken from a believing heart carries energy. That energy is charged by your inner state—faith, peace, and love amplify it; doubt, anger, and fear distort it.

This is why Jesus often withdrew to pray before performing miracles: He was tuning His human heart to the Father's frequency.

To operate in Kingdom power, your heart must be trained to vibrate with **faith coherence**—the spiritual rhythm where emotion, belief, and Spirit move as one.

Faith coherence is achieved through worship, meditation on the Word, and stillness in God's presence. These practices synchronize your internal rhythm with divine reality. When that alignment occurs, prayer stops being an act of asking and becomes an act of releasing what already exists in heaven.

Faith is not convincing God—it is agreeing with Him.

When your heart transmits faith, heaven recognizes its own frequency and responds.

End-of-Chapter Framework

Self-Reflection Questions

1. What frequency does my heart currently emit—faith, fear, or uncertainty?
2. Do my words and emotions vibrate with confidence in God's promises?
3. How can I cultivate inner coherence between what I believe and what I speak?

Devotional Insight (Redirected, Readjusted, Set Aright, Increased in Holiness)

The Spirit redirects your faith from striving to resting.

He readjusts your energy, aligning your emotions with divine peace.

He sets aright your spiritual frequency, tuning your heart to heaven's harmony.

As holiness increases, faith ceases to be effort and becomes effortless resonance with God.

Affirmation of Faith

"My heart vibrates with the frequency of faith.

I am tuned to the sound of heaven and aligned with the power of God's Word.

What He has spoken, I believe. What I believe, I manifest.

His will flows through me as light and life to the world."

Prayer of Alignment

Father, tune my heart to the rhythm of Your faith.

Silence every vibration of fear, doubt, and disbelief.

Let my emotions, words, and thoughts harmonize with Your truth.

May my faith broadcast Your presence and draw heaven's reality into my world.

In Jesus' name, Amen.

Scripture Anchors

- *Hebrews 11:1* — "Faith is the substance of things hoped for."
- *Mark 11:23* — "If you believe in your heart… it will be done."

Key Takeaways

- Faith is a divine frequency released through the believing heart.
- The heart transmits energy that aligns with heaven's order or earthly fear.
- Coherent faith creates manifestation; divided faith creates delay.
- Rest, worship, and alignment tune the heart to divine frequency.

Call to Action

Spend five minutes in deep, slow breathing and quiet worship.

With each exhale, release fear; with each inhale, receive faith.

As you do, visualize your heart glowing with the light of belief—expanding outward as a wave of divine energy.

Speak aloud:

"My faith aligns with God's truth; my heart emits heaven's frequency."

Then go about your day carrying that atmosphere—the sound of faith changing your world.

CHAPTER TWELVE

The Battle of Frequencies: When Faith Meets Fear

"For God has not given us a spirit of fear, but of power and of love and of a sound mind." — 2 Timothy 1:7 (AMP)

Part A — Revelation and Definition

Every human being lives in a constant exchange of energy—spiritual, emotional, and mental. The heart is the generator of that energy, releasing signals that either harmonize with heaven (faith) or resonate with darkness (fear).

When God created humanity, He designed the heart to vibrate with divine frequency—love, peace, and faith. But after sin entered the world, the human heart began broadcasting a mixed signal: light and shadow, trust and doubt, peace and panic.

This is the **battle of frequencies**—the inner war between what God says and what fear whispers.

Faith and fear cannot occupy the same space. One builds; the other breaks.

Faith says, *"It is finished."*

Fear says, *"What if it fails?"*

Faith aligns with heaven's certainty.

Fear echoes the uncertainty of a fallen world.

The heart is the battleground because it controls the transmission of both.

When faith is strong, the heart's field expands—radiating peace, attracting clarity, and aligning with divine order.

When fear takes over, the field contracts—creating anxiety, confusion, and physical tension.

The energy of faith and the energy of fear cannot harmonize. They produce interference, static, and spiritual fatigue. The key to victory is not to fight fear directly but to **retune the heart** to its original frequency—perfect love.

1 John 4:18 declares, *"Perfect love casts out fear."* Love is the highest frequency of heaven, and fear cannot coexist in its presence.

Part B — Kingdom Insight and Application

Faith and fear both require imagination; both create worlds.

Faith envisions what God has promised and manifests it through trust.

Fear imagines what the enemy threatens and manifests it through worry.

Whichever image the heart embraces becomes the world you experience.

That is why Jesus often said, *"Do not be afraid—only believe."* He was not dismissing emotion but instructing alignment. Fear drains energy; faith directs it.

The **battle of frequencies** is won not by emotional control but by spiritual coherence. When your heart is aligned with the Spirit of God, fear's vibration dissolves naturally. The light doesn't argue with darkness—it simply shines, and darkness flees.

To overcome fear's interference, three spiritual recalibrations must occur:

1. **Return to Presence** – Fear thrives in imagined futures; faith lives in the eternal now. When you bring your awareness back to God's presence in this moment, the heart's frequency stabilizes.

2. **Release Control** – Fear grows in the soil of self-reliance. Surrendering control restores flow. When you trust God's sovereignty, your heart re-tunes to divine rhythm.

3. **Reinforce Love** – Love is the original frequency of faith. Speak love, think love, act in love—and fear loses its voltage.

When you live in alignment, even challenges begin to serve you. The same storm that once frightened you becomes a current of growth when the heart stays anchored in peace.

Every decision you make releases energy into your environment. Choose faith, and the air around you changes. Choose fear, and confusion multiplies. But the moment you remember who rules your heart, the storm within obeys.

Jesus demonstrated this on the Sea of Galilee. While His disciples panicked, He slept—fully synchronized with heaven's calm. When He awoke, He didn't fight the wind; He *spoke peace.* The external storm responded to the frequency of His inner stillness.

You carry that same authority. When your heart vibrates with peace, fear has no home.

End-of-Chapter Framework

Self-Reflection Questions

1. What fears have recently interfered with my faith frequency?
2. Do I spend more energy imagining what could go wrong or what God has promised will go right?
3. How can I retune my heart to perfect love today?

Devotional Insight (Redirected, Readjusted, Set Aright, Increased in Holiness)

The Spirit redirects your focus from the storm to the stillness.

He readjusts your inner frequency, aligning it with divine love.

He sets aright the flow of energy between your heart and spirit.

As holiness increases, fear loses resonance and peace becomes your atmosphere.

Affirmation of Faith

"My heart vibrates with the sound of heaven.

Fear has no frequency in me.

Love governs my being, faith directs my path, and peace surrounds my world."

Prayer of Realignment

Father, I choose Your frequency of faith.

Silence every vibration of fear within me.

Let Your perfect love cast out every shadow.

Teach my heart to echo heaven's calm even in life's storms.

May my presence bring peace to others as Your presence brings peace to me.

In Jesus' name, Amen.

Scripture Anchors

- *2 Timothy 1:7* — "God has not given us a spirit of fear, but of power, love, and a sound mind."
- *1 John 4:18* — "Perfect love casts out fear."

Key Takeaways

- Faith and fear are opposing spiritual frequencies.
- Fear collapses energy; faith expands it.
- Love is the highest frequency that dissolves fear.
- Alignment with God's presence restores peace and power.

Call to Action

Sit quietly with one hand on your heart.

Breathe in deeply, saying, "God is here."

Exhale slowly, saying, "Fear must go."

Repeat until your heartbeat slows and peace rises.

Then declare aloud:

"My heart is tuned to the frequency of faith. I live in the rhythm of divine love."

CHAPTER THIRTEEN

The Rhythm of Peace: Living in Divine Coherence

"And the peace of God, which transcends all understanding, will guard your hearts and your minds in Christ Jesus." — Philippians 4:7 (AMP)

Part A — Revelation and Definition

Peace is not the absence of conflict; it is the **presence of divine order**.

It is the sacred rhythm of heaven resonating through the human heart—where everything within moves in agreement with God's will.

In Hebrew, the word for peace, **shalom**, means far more than calm or stillness. It means *wholeness, completeness, harmony, and alignment with divine purpose.* When the Bible declares that God's peace will "guard your hearts and minds," it is describing a living force—*an energy field of balance* that protects and governs every dimension of your being.

The heart produces rhythm physically through its beat, but spiritually, it produces rhythm through belief. When your belief aligns with truth, the rhythm is steady; when you are anxious or fearful, the rhythm becomes erratic.

The Spirit's work in you is to synchronize your internal rhythm with heaven's—this is what we call **divine coherence**.

Divine coherence occurs when the spirit, heart, and mind operate as one organism under the guidance of peace. It is a state where emotional turbulence ceases, mental clarity returns, and physical vitality flows.

This is why Jesus said, *"My peace I give to you—not as the world gives."* (John 14:27) The world offers temporary calm through control; the Kingdom offers eternal peace through surrender.

You were created to live in rhythm with the heartbeat of God.

Part B — Kingdom Insight and Application

Divine coherence is both a spiritual and physiological reality.

Studies in neurocardiology confirm that when the heart enters a state of coherence—meaning it beats in a smooth, ordered rhythm—the brain synchronizes, emotional stability increases, and the body heals faster.

Spiritually, this reflects what happens when the soul aligns with God's peace.

Every system—mental, emotional, physical—comes into divine order.

The peace of God, then, is more than a feeling; it is **spiritual architecture**—a design of harmony between heaven and humanity.

To maintain this rhythm of peace, three spiritual practices are essential:

1. **Stillness Before God** – Peace requires space to breathe. When you pause in His presence, your heart entrains to His rhythm. Silence is not emptiness; it is recalibration.

2. **Obedience in Faith** – Peace flows where there is agreement. Disobedience disrupts rhythm because it pulls you out of harmony with divine instruction. Obedience restores resonance.

3. **Worship as Alignment** – Worship tunes the heart. It transforms chaotic energy into holy harmony. Every time you lift your voice in worship, your inner rhythm realigns with heaven's pulse.

Divine coherence means that your outer life mirrors your inner peace. You move, speak, and decide in sync with the Spirit. Even when challenges arise, your equilibrium remains.

Peace is not passive—it is **protective**. It is the spiritual armor that shields the heart from emotional invasion.

That is why Paul said, *"Let the peace of God rule in your hearts."* (Colossians 3:15) The word *rule* means "to act as an umpire." Peace decides what stays and what must go.

When peace rules, confusion cannot stay.

When peace rules, anxiety loses access.

When peace rules, divine order reigns.

The believer walking in divine coherence becomes a living example of stability in a chaotic world. Your calm becomes contagious. Your presence releases peace that shifts atmospheres, because your heart has become a rhythmic reflection of heaven.

End-of-Chapter Framework

Self-Reflection Questions

1. Do I experience peace as an occasional feeling or as a continual rhythm?
2. What thoughts or habits interrupt my inner coherence with God's Spirit?
3. How can I cultivate daily stillness to maintain divine rhythm in my heart?

Devotional Insight (Redirected, Readjusted, Set Aright, Increased in Holiness)

The Spirit redirects your pace to match heaven's rhythm.

He readjusts your emotional flow, replacing chaos with order.

He sets aright your spiritual heartbeat, aligning it with divine timing.

As holiness increases, peace becomes your permanent atmosphere—not a momentary relief.

Affirmation of Faith

"My heart beats with the rhythm of heaven.

The peace of God rules within me and orders my every step.

No storm can disrupt my harmony, for I dwell in divine coherence.

I live, move, and have my being in His peace."

Prayer of Alignment

Father, teach my heart to live in the rhythm of Your peace.

Where I have hurried ahead or lagged behind, bring me back into divine timing.

Let Your shalom guard every part of me—spirit, mind, and body.

Make my life a living symphony of harmony, health, and holiness.

In Jesus' name, Amen.

Scripture Anchors

- *Philippians 4:7* — "The peace of God will guard your hearts and minds."
- *John 14:27* — "My peace I give to you."

Key Takeaways

- Peace is divine order, not mere calm.
- The heart's rhythm reflects spiritual alignment or disruption.
- Stillness, obedience, and worship sustain divine coherence.
- Peace protects and governs the entire being under God's authority.

Call to Action

Take a few moments today to synchronize your breathing with gratitude.

As you inhale, whisper, "Your peace fills me."

As you exhale, say, "Your peace flows through me."

Repeat until your inner stillness deepens.

Throughout the day, walk in this rhythm—your steps guided by the unseen heartbeat of God.

CHAPTER FOURTEEN

The Anatomy of Wholeness: When Spirit, Mind, and Body Heal as One

"May your whole spirit and soul and body be kept blameless at the coming of our Lord Jesus Christ." — *1 Thessalonians 5:23 (AMP)*

Part A — Revelation and Definition

Wholeness is the original state of creation. Before the fall, every part of Adam's being—his spirit, mind, and body—functioned in perfect alignment under the rule of divine presence. There was no separation, no disease, no inner conflict. He lived in uninterrupted harmony with his Creator.

Sin fractured that unity. The spirit was disconnected from God, the mind darkened, and the body subjected to corruption. Yet through Christ, God initiated the restoration of that original design. Redemption is not only forgiveness—it is **integration**, the healing of the fragmented self.

To be made whole means to be **reconnected**—to return to divine order where every part of your being communicates freely and functions under one purpose: to glorify God.

The anatomy of wholeness has three interdependent dimensions:

1. **The Spirit** — the breath of God within, the source of divine identity.
2. **The Mind (Soul)** — the processor of belief, emotion, and decision.
3. **The Body** — the physical vessel that carries out divine intention on earth.

When these three operate independently, life becomes fragmented. But when they come into alignment under the authority of the Holy Spirit, **healing flows naturally**—spiritual, emotional, and physical.

Wholeness, then, is not achieved by effort but by **agreement**.

It is the heart's surrender to divine order, allowing the Spirit's life to circulate freely through every part of your being.

This is the meaning behind Jesus' words to the healed leper: *"Your faith has made you whole."* (Luke 17:19) The man was not only cleansed physically but restored internally—his faith reconnected him to divine flow.

Part B — Kingdom Insight and Application

Every system in the human body reflects a spiritual principle.

The **circulatory system** mirrors the movement of the Spirit—life flowing through the heart to nourish every cell.

The **nervous system** mirrors the mind—carrying signals of thought, instruction, and command.

The **immune system** mirrors spiritual discernment—identifying what belongs and rejecting what does not.

When any of these systems are disrupted, disease occurs. The same is true spiritually: when your spirit, mind, or body falls out of alignment with God's rhythm, imbalance manifests.

The key to restoration is **integration**—the reuniting of all parts under the governance of peace.

The Spirit of God is the master physician who heals not just symptoms but separation.

Divine healing is not only a miracle—it is a process of reconnection. It happens as:

- The **spirit** reconnects to God through intimacy.
- The **mind** renews its patterns through truth.
- The **body** responds in strength as peace flows from within.

Many seek healing of the body while neglecting the mind or spirit. True wholeness, however, is an ecosystem of unity.

A healed heart produces a peaceful mind.

A peaceful mind signals the body to release tension.

A relaxed body allows energy to flow, and the Spirit's life moves unhindered.

This is why Jesus often said, *"Your faith has made you whole,"* rather than simply, *"You are healed."* He was restoring divine order to the entire being.

To live in wholeness is to understand that health is holy. Every breath, thought, and action becomes worship when all three parts of you operate in harmony.

In this state, sickness loses its authority, anxiety loses its grip, and confusion finds no resting place. You become an instrument of divine vitality—radiant from the inside out.

End-of-Chapter Framework

Self-Reflection Questions

1. Which part of my being—spirit, mind, or body—has been out of alignment with God's rhythm?
2. Do I treat healing as a spiritual event or as an ongoing integration process?
3. How can I invite the Holy Spirit to restore communication between all parts of my being?

Devotional Insight (Redirected, Readjusted, Set Aright, Increased in Holiness)

The Spirit redirects your pursuit from relief to restoration.

He readjusts your understanding of healing—from momentary miracles to continual integration.

He sets aright your inner systems, reconnecting spirit, mind, and body as one vessel of glory.

As holiness increases, life flows freely and effortlessly through you.

Affirmation of Faith

"My spirit is united with God.

My mind is renewed by His truth.

My body is strengthened by His presence.

I live whole, healed, and harmonized in His divine order."

Prayer of Wholeness

Father, I yield every part of myself to You—spirit, mind, and body.

Restore the divine connections that sin or stress have disrupted.

Let Your peace flow through my nervous system, Your Word renew my mind, and Your Spirit strengthen my body.

May every breath I take testify that I am whole in You.

In Jesus' name, Amen.

Scripture Anchors

- *1 Thessalonians 5:23* — "May your whole spirit, soul, and body be kept blameless."
- *Luke 17:19* — "Your faith has made you whole."

Key Takeaways

- Wholeness is divine integration—spirit, mind, and body working as one.
- Healing begins with reconnection to God's Spirit.
- True health flows from alignment, not effort.
- Every believer is designed to live as a unified expression of God's life.

Call to Action

Today, take a few moments to speak alignment over yourself:

"My spirit hears, my heart believes, my mind agrees, and my body responds."

Visualize light flowing from your heart through your entire being.

Each breath is restoration; each moment is integration.

Wholeness is your inheritance—walk in it with confidence and gratitude.

CHAPTER FIFTEEN

The Healing Intelligence of the Heart: How God's Spirit Regenerates Life from Within

"The Spirit of God has made me, and the breath of the Almighty gives me life." — *Job 33:4 (AMP)*

Part A — Revelation and Definition

The human heart is not only the center of emotion and circulation; it is a **biological and spiritual intelligence**—a divine instrument of renewal.

When God created humanity, He placed His breath within the heart, giving it the power to sustain, communicate, and regenerate life.

Science now confirms what Scripture declared long ago: the heart possesses its own neural network—a "heart-brain" capable of learning, remembering, and sending signals that influence the entire body. But beyond biology lies divine mystery.

The **healing intelligence of the heart** is the manifestation of the Spirit of God dwelling within—the continual flow of divine energy that restores what life's strain has fractured. The same Spirit that raised Christ from the dead now dwells in you (Romans 8:11), and that Spirit works from the inside out, regenerating every dimension of your being.

When the heart is at peace, its electromagnetic field radiates harmony, communicating balance to the brain and coherence to every cell.

When the heart is troubled, that field becomes chaotic, and dissonance spreads throughout the body.

Healing, therefore, begins not with medication alone but with **spiritual recalibration**—returning the heart to its original harmony with the Spirit of God.

This divine intelligence works quietly and continually. Every beat of the heart is an echo of creation's rhythm, a reminder that life flows from a spiritual source. The heart's intelligence is not self-derived; it is the Spirit's wisdom expressing itself through physical design.

The moment the believer surrenders to divine peace, the heart begins to "remember" its sacred programming—to heal, to harmonize, and to restore.

Part B — Kingdom Insight and Application

When Scripture declares, *"A merry heart does good like medicine"* (Proverbs 17:22), it is revealing a profound spiritual law: emotional and spiritual harmony produce physical regeneration.

Joy, gratitude, forgiveness, and love activate the heart's healing intelligence, releasing waves of coherence that repair both body and soul.

The Spirit's healing process follows this divine pattern:

1. **Illumination** — The Spirit brings awareness to the area of imbalance.

2. **Surrender** — The believer releases control, inviting God's flow.

3. **Regeneration** — Life-force energy, powered by divine Spirit, renews every system from the inside out.

In the Kingdom, healing is not an event—it is a rhythm. Every time you breathe, worship, forgive, or choose faith over fear, you participate in this rhythm of regeneration.

The heart's intelligence also governs **memory healing**—the restoration of emotional wounds stored in the body. Each unresolved hurt creates energetic residue that disturbs flow. But when the Spirit brings those memories to light and the believer releases them through prayer and forgiveness, energy flow is restored, and physical vitality follows.

The power that raised Jesus from the dead is resurrection intelligence—the ultimate form of divine coherence. It does not merely revive what is dying; it **reprograms** the living to align with eternal life. That same power is at work in every believer's heart today.

When you meditate on truth, worship in spirit, and breathe in peace, you are activating the heart's healing intelligence. Cells respond. Hormones balance. The body begins to mirror the wholeness of the spirit.

This is why the psalmist could say, *"He restores my soul."* Restoration is not abstract—it is physical, emotional, and spiritual recalibration into divine harmony.

Healing, then, is not something you pursue; it is something you **allow**. It begins when resistance ends and divine intelligence takes over.

End-of-Chapter Framework

Self-Reflection Questions

1. What emotions or memories still disrupt the rhythm of my heart's peace?
2. How often do I intentionally allow the Spirit of God to breathe life into my being?
3. What would it mean for me to live daily from the intelligence of a healed heart?

Devotional Insight (Redirected, Readjusted, Set Aright, Increased in Holiness)

The Spirit redirects your attention from symptoms to source.

He readjusts your flow, teaching you that healing begins with peace.

He sets aright the inner communication between spirit and body.

As holiness increases, divine intelligence awakens within you, renewing every cell with light.

Affirmation of Faith

"The Spirit of God within me renews my life.

My heart is a channel of divine healing and wisdom.

Peace flows through my veins; joy strengthens my cells.

I am continually regenerated by the breath of God."

Prayer of Renewal

Father, I receive Your breath of life afresh.

Heal the hidden places of my heart where stress, grief, or fear once ruled.

Let Your Spirit restore harmony to my mind, body, and emotions.

Awaken the intelligence You placed within me at creation.

May my entire being reflect the vitality of Your resurrection power.

In Jesus' name, Amen.

Scripture Anchors

- *Job 33:4* — "The Spirit of God has made me, and the breath of the Almighty gives me life."
- *Romans 8:11* — "The Spirit who raised Jesus from the dead will also give life to your mortal bodies."

Key Takeaways

- The heart carries divine intelligence and communicates directly with the Spirit.
- Emotional and spiritual harmony release the body's natural capacity to heal.
- Joy, gratitude, and forgiveness activate the regenerative flow of life.
- The Spirit's presence is the ultimate healing force within you.

Call to Action

Take a few minutes each morning to sit in quiet gratitude.

Place your hand over your heart and whisper,

"Spirit of God, breathe in me."

Visualize His light expanding through your chest, radiating into every cell.

As you exhale, release all tension, pain, and fear.

Repeat until peace and energy return.

This is how divine intelligence renews your life—one breath, one beat, one surrender at a time.

CHAPTER SIXTEEN

The Electromagnetic Signature of Glory: How God's Energy Marks and Protects the Believer

"But we all, with unveiled face, beholding as in a mirror the glory of the Lord, are being transformed into the same image from glory to glory." — 2 Corinthians 3:18 (AMP)

Part A — Revelation and Definition

Glory is not an abstract glow—it is the **energetic signature of God's presence** expressed through His creation.

Every living being carries a field of energy, but those filled with the Spirit of God emit a frequency unlike any other: the radiant energy of divine glory.

This **electromagnetic signature** is heaven's identification mark—a spiritual imprint that testifies, *"This one belongs to Me."*

In Scripture, glory (*kabod* in Hebrew) literally means *weight* or *substance*. It is the tangible density of God's presence. Wherever His glory manifests, there is power, protection, and transformation.

When the human heart becomes His dwelling place, that same glory takes residence within. It begins to emanate outward—through words, touch, presence, and even atmosphere.

Moses reflected this reality when he descended from Mount Sinai. His face shone with light because his heart had absorbed divine radiation.

Likewise, when Stephen was filled with the Spirit, his face "appeared as the face of an angel." (Acts 6:15)

This was the **signature of glory**—the visible evidence of invisible communion.

Every believer who abides in continual fellowship with God becomes a living transmitter of this light. The Spirit not only dwells within but also expands around, creating a sphere of holy energy that influences the environment and repels spiritual darkness.

That sphere is not imagination—it is the divine field of glory that surrounds those who walk in truth.

Part B — Kingdom Insight and Application

The electromagnetic signature of glory is both **transformational** and **protective**.

Transformational because it changes you from the inside out; protective because it establishes a boundary of divine energy that the enemy cannot penetrate.

Isaiah 60:2 declares, *"Darkness shall cover the earth, and deep darkness the people; but the Lord will arise over you, and His glory will be seen upon you."*

This prophecy describes more than symbolic light—it reveals the divine contrast between the energy of fear and the frequency of glory.

When a believer walks in purity of heart, their electromagnetic field harmonizes with the Spirit's light. That resonance becomes a **spiritual shield**—repelling fear, absorbing chaos, and restoring balance.

The power of this field does not depend on effort but on alignment.

When your heart is filled with worship, gratitude, and faith, your energy field expands—strong, luminous, and coherent.

When your heart is weighed down with bitterness or sin, the field contracts—dimmed and vulnerable.

The secret to sustaining the glory field is continual communion. The more you behold His face, the stronger your radiance becomes. The more you walk in love, the wider your field of peace extends.

This radiant glory is also a form of divine communication. The world senses it before hearing it.

People feel calm, conviction, or healing in your presence because the glory surrounding you carries God's living frequency.

It becomes a **signature**—unique to every believer but consistent in essence: light, peace, and holiness.

This is the mystery of transformation from "glory to glory." The heart, as it beholds the Lord, continually absorbs His energy until your entire being vibrates with His likeness.

The glory that marks you also guards you.

It is your **spiritual armor**—a living field that no weapon can penetrate, no curse can attach to, and no darkness can extinguish.

When your electromagnetic signature bears the imprint of glory, you do not just carry His presence—you *become* an extension of His radiance in the earth.

End-of-Chapter Framework

Self-Reflection Questions

1. How conscious am I of the presence of God radiating from within me daily?
2. Do I carry the atmosphere of peace and light that marks me as His own?
3. What practices strengthen my communion and expand my field of glory?

Devotional Insight (Redirected, Readjusted, Set Aright, Increased in Holiness)

The Spirit redirects your attention from external warfare to internal radiance.

He readjusts your perception, showing that divine protection flows from divine presence.

He sets aright your inner atmosphere, transforming chaos into light.

As holiness increases, your glory field becomes a mantle of peace that no darkness can touch.

Affirmation of Faith

"The glory of God radiates through me.

I am marked by His light and protected by His presence.

My heart emanates peace; my life reflects His power.

No darkness can invade what His glory surrounds."

Prayer of Consecration

Father, I thank You for the glory You have placed within me.

Let it expand as I worship, love, and walk in obedience.

Mark me with Your light and shield me with Your presence.

May everyone who enters my atmosphere encounter Your peace.

Let my life become a radiant witness of Your eternal power.

In Jesus' name, Amen.

Scripture Anchors

- *2 Corinthians 3:18* — "We are transformed into the same image from glory to glory."
- *Isaiah 60:2* — "The Lord will arise over you, and His glory will be seen upon you."

Key Takeaways

- The glory of God is a tangible energy signature that emanates from the believer's heart.
- Purity and worship expand this field; sin and fear constrict it.
- The glory field transforms, protects, and communicates divine presence.

- Every believer is uniquely marked by heaven's light.

Call to Action

Each morning, declare aloud:

"The glory of the Lord rises upon me today."

Visualize a radiant field of golden light expanding from your heart—six feet, then twelve, then beyond—filled with peace and holiness.

Move through your day aware of this shield of glory.

Let your presence carry His energy of healing, calm, and victory wherever you go.

CHAPTER SEVENTEEN

The Heart as a Portal of Light: Bridging Heaven and Earth Within

"Your eye is a lamp that provides light for your body. When your eye is healthy, your whole body is filled with light." — Matthew 6:22 (NLT)

Part A — Revelation and Definition

Every act of creation begins with light. When God said, *"Let there be light,"* He did not simply ignite physical illumination—He released **spiritual consciousness**, the energy of divine awareness that brings form to the formless.

That same creative light dwells within the human heart.

The heart was designed as the **portal**—a divine threshold where the eternal touches the temporal, where the unseen realm of Spirit flows into the visible dimension of matter.

When the Spirit of God enters the believer, He reopens this inner gate that was closed through sin. The heart, once darkened by separation, becomes a radiant corridor through which the glory of heaven shines.

Jesus declared, *"The Kingdom of God is within you."* (Luke 17:21)

The Kingdom is not distant—it is *dimensional*, operating from within the human vessel as divine light radiating outward.

In the ancient Hebraic understanding, the heart was viewed as the "lamp of the inner man." It was believed that God's wisdom entered through the spirit and was projected outward through the heart, giving light to the mind, the eyes, and the body.

When the heart is pure, this light flows freely. When the heart is defiled, the portal narrows, and darkness spreads.

Thus, holiness is not restriction—it is **expansion of light**. The purer the heart, the wider the opening through which God's glory can flow.

A sanctified heart becomes a luminous gateway through which heaven communicates, creates, and heals. You are not merely a vessel—you are a living conduit between worlds, carrying divine radiance into earthly expression.

Part B — Kingdom Insight and Application

To live as a *portal of light* means to live consciously aware that heaven is active within you.

Every thought, word, and act becomes a potential transmission of divine energy. When your heart remains surrendered, the flow of heaven remains uninterrupted.

This is what Jesus meant when He said, *"Out of your belly shall flow rivers of living water."* (John 7:38) Those rivers are not physical—they are spiritual currents of light, love, and life flowing through the sanctified heart.

The *portal of light* opens wider through three spiritual disciplines:

1. **Purity of Intention** — A pure heart is transparent, allowing God's light to pass through without distortion. Guard your motives and remove all self-glory. The less of self, the more of God's shine.

2. **Continual Communion** — Every moment of prayer, worship, or gratitude strengthens your inner circuitry. The connection deepens; the current of glory flows stronger.

3. **Active Compassion** — Love is the key that opens the gate. Every act of kindness amplifies light, transforming the heart from a window to a radiant beacon.

When you live in this awareness, you begin to notice that your surroundings respond to your inner light. People feel peace in your presence. Environments shift when you enter the room. The Kingdom expands through your energy of love and faith.

This is not mystical imagination—it is Kingdom science. The light of God is measurable, transmittable, and transformative. The believer's heart becomes the *bridge* between the unseen Spirit and the seen creation, carrying revelation, healing, and divine order wherever you go.

The heart is not just a place where God resides; it is a **portal through which He flows**.

The more you yield, the more He shines.

The more you love, the more He manifests.

The more you believe, the more heaven becomes visible on earth through you.

You are God's living lamp—His light in human form.

End-of-Chapter Framework

Self-Reflection Questions

1. Do I see my heart as a vessel that contains God or as a portal through which He flows?
2. What thoughts, habits, or emotions dim the radiance of divine light within me?
3. How can I expand my heart's openness to manifest heaven's light on earth?

Devotional Insight (Redirected, Readjusted, Set Aright, Increased in Holiness)

The Spirit redirects your understanding of the heart from container to conduit.

He readjusts your awareness from limited worship to living flow.

He sets aright your consciousness, revealing heaven's nearness within.

As holiness increases, your heart becomes a blazing portal of divine radiance.

Affirmation of Faith

"My heart is a gateway of divine light.

Heaven flows through me to touch the earth.

I am a living lamp of God's glory—pure, radiant, and whole.

Through me, His light brings healing, peace, and transformation."

Prayer of Illumination

Father of Light,

Open the portal of my heart fully to Your glory.

Remove every shadow that restricts the flow of Your presence.

Let Your Kingdom radiate through me in every word and deed.

May my life shine as proof that heaven is here, alive within me.

In Jesus' name, Amen.

Scripture Anchors

- *Matthew 6:22* — "When your eye is healthy, your whole body is filled with light."
- *Luke 17:21* — "The Kingdom of God is within you."

Key Takeaways

- The sanctified heart is the portal where heaven and earth meet.
- Light is the substance of God's glory, transmitted through purity and love.
- Every believer is designed to radiate divine energy into the world.
- The greater the surrender, the wider the portal and the stronger the light.

Call to Action

Begin your day by visualizing your heart as a radiant doorway of light.

Say aloud:

"Father, let Your light flow through me today."

Picture that light expanding outward—touching your home, workplace, and community.

Then live as one who knows: wherever you walk, heaven walks with you.

CHAPTER EIGHTEEN

The Magnetic Field of Love: Drawing Miracles, People, and Purpose into Divine Alignment

"Above all, clothe yourselves with love, which binds us all together in perfect harmony." — Colossians 3:14 (NLT)

Part A — Revelation and Definition

Love is not only an emotion; it is a **spiritual magnetism**—the field of divine attraction that governs every dimension of Kingdom life.

Everything God does flows through the frequency of love. Creation itself is love expressed as light, life, and motion.

The Bible declares, *"God is love."* (1 John 4:8) Therefore, love is not something God gives—it is what He is. It is His nature, His law, and His essence.

When the believer abides in love, they align with the most powerful energy in the universe. Love harmonizes opposites, dissolves resistance, and draws all things into divine order.

The **magnetic field of love** originates in the heart—the same heart that is the portal of light and the dwelling place of the Spirit.

When love reigns within, the heart emits a strong, coherent field that attracts the resources, relationships, and revelations necessary for your purpose.

This is not emotional attraction but **spiritual alignment**. Love calls into being what fear repels. Love unites what pride divides. Love opens doors that intellect cannot.

It is the current that carries miracles into manifestation.

Love's magnetism is selfless, pure, and steady. It seeks not possession but expression. The moment the heart chooses love—especially in the face of opposition—it begins to release a vibration that reorganizes reality according to heaven's pattern.

This is why Jesus taught that the greatest commandment is to *"love the Lord your God with all your heart"* and *"love your neighbor as yourself."*

Love is the very architecture of the Kingdom. It is the invisible force that connects the seen and unseen realms into one perfect flow.

Part B — Kingdom Insight and Application

When divine love flows freely through the heart, it creates a **magnetic field**—a living aura of peace and favor that naturally attracts what belongs to your destiny.

This field is not manipulation; it is manifestation through resonance.

Three principles govern the magnetic field of love:

1. **Love Aligns Energy.**
   Where there is love, there is coherence. Relationships flourish, creativity multiplies, and divine timing accelerates. Love synchronizes your energy with the rhythm of heaven.

2. **Love Heals Separation.**

    Every division—whether in body, mind, or relationship—begins to heal when love enters. Love bridges gaps that logic cannot cross. It restores connection and closes the distance between pain and peace.

3. **Love Attracts Purpose.**

    The more love you release, the more divine opportunities find you. Love magnetizes everything needed to fulfill your calling because it mirrors the heart of God, who is the source of all purpose.

When you walk in love, you no longer chase destiny—**destiny recognizes you**.

Like iron drawn to a magnet, the resources of heaven align with your vibration of compassion, gratitude, and faith.

This is why miracles often happen in environments of love. Jesus was moved with compassion, and healing flowed. Love opened the channel for power to operate.

The absence of love, on the other hand, creates resistance. Resentment, jealousy, and fear distort the field, repelling what God has prepared.

The heart's magnetism weakens when contaminated by bitterness or self-pity.

To restore the field, return to the posture of love.

Forgive freely. Bless intentionally. Worship fully.

As you do, divine order returns, and what once seemed delayed begins to find you again.

Love is the **currency of the Kingdom**—and it never fails.

End-of-Chapter Framework

Self-Reflection Questions

1. Am I radiating love in my words, thoughts, and presence—or am I carrying hidden resistance?
2. Who or what in my life needs to be forgiven so that my heart's field can expand again?
3. How can I intentionally express divine love to attract greater alignment with God's purpose?

Devotional Insight (Redirected, Readjusted, Set Aright, Increased in Holiness)

The Spirit redirects your energy from striving to radiating.

He readjusts your posture from defensiveness to openness.

He sets aright your understanding—love is not weakness; it is divine strength in motion.

As holiness increases, love's magnetism intensifies, drawing every miracle and divine connection into your orbit.

Affirmation of Faith

"My heart radiates divine love.

Everything in harmony with God's will is drawn to me.

I live in the current of compassion, peace, and purpose.

Love governs my path, multiplies my blessings, and manifests my destiny."

Prayer of Alignment

Father, saturate my heart with Your perfect love.

Cleanse it from all fear, pride, and bitterness.

Let Your love flow through me as a magnetic field of peace and healing.

Draw to me only what reflects Your purpose, and let everything else fall away.

Make my life a living testimony of love's power to transform.

In Jesus' name, Amen.

Scripture Anchors

- *Colossians 3:14* — "Love binds us all together in perfect harmony."
- *1 John 4:8* — "God is love."
- *Mark 12:30-31* — "Love the Lord your God ... and your neighbor as yourself."

Key Takeaways

- Love is divine magnetism—the energy of creation itself.
- The heart's magnetic field expands with gratitude, worship, and forgiveness.
- Love heals, aligns, and attracts everything necessary for divine purpose.

- Living in love transforms your atmosphere into a Kingdom frequency.

Call to Action

Take a moment to close your eyes and breathe deeply.

Visualize your heart glowing with warm light, expanding outward with every breath.

Whisper:

"I choose love in every thought, every word, every moment."

As you go through your day, observe how peace follows you, how kindness multiplies, and how divine opportunities begin to approach you without strain.

That is the magnetic field of love—Heaven's current moving through your heart.

CHAPTER NINETEEN

The Energy of Forgiveness: Releasing the Past and Restoring Spiritual Flow

"Be kind and compassionate to one another, forgiving each other, just as in Christ God forgave you." — Ephesians 4:32 (NIV)

Part A — Revelation and Definition

Forgiveness is one of the most powerful **energetic transactions** in the Kingdom.

It is the process by which divine love dissolves emotional residue, spiritual blockage, and energetic tension caused by pain, betrayal, or disappointment.

In Kingdom terms, forgiveness is **the cleansing of the heart's field** so that the current of the Spirit can once again move without obstruction.

When unforgiveness lingers, the heart's magnetic field constricts.

Bitterness, resentment, and judgment create interference in the flow of life-energy.

It is like sediment in a river—the water still exists, but it cannot move freely.

God's Spirit still resides within, but His current becomes muffled beneath layers of emotional debris.

Forgiveness is not amnesia. It is **alignment**.

It means releasing the emotional charge that binds you to the memory of offense, returning your inner vibration to peace, and allowing the Spirit to heal both memory and meaning.

Jesus spoke of forgiveness as a spiritual law: *"If you forgive others their trespasses, your heavenly Father will also forgive you."* (Matthew 6:14)

In that statement, He revealed not a condition for acceptance but a **principle of resonance**—only a forgiven heart can vibrate with the frequency of divine mercy.

When you forgive, you **reset your energetic system** to grace.

You return to divine rhythm, where your spirit and heart can once again communicate clearly.

Unforgiveness, by contrast, drains spiritual vitality.

It anchors you in the past, keeping your energy tied to moments God already redeemed.

Every time the offense is replayed, the heart emits a discordant signal that keeps heaven's flow restricted.

Healing cannot manifest where resentment circulates.

Forgiveness breaks that cycle.

It frees the offender from your judgment—and it frees you from their energetic imprint.

It is the divine detox of the soul.

The Multi-Layered Anatomy of Forgiveness

1. **Spiritual Dimension — Divine Exchange**
   Forgiveness begins in the spirit. You surrender the right to

vengeance and place justice into God's hands. This act re-establishes covenant order—God as Judge, you as vessel of grace.

2. **Emotional Dimension — Energetic Cleansing**
   Tears, prayer, and honest confession act like spiritual solvents. They dissolve emotional toxins, allowing peace to wash through your nervous system.

3. **Cognitive Dimension — Renewal of Perception**
   The mind must agree with the spirit. As you release the offense, you begin to see the situation through redemptive eyes. The story changes from *"what they did to me"* to *"what God healed in me."*

4. **Physical Dimension — Somatic Freedom**
   Medical science affirms what Scripture has long declared: unforgiveness breeds tension, fatigue, and disease. Forgiveness literally lightens the body's load, recalibrating hormones and immune function.

Thus, forgiveness is not weakness—it is **energetic mastery**. It is reclaiming dominion over your inner atmosphere.

Part B — Kingdom Insight and Application

The heart is both an **emotional processor** and a **spiritual transmitter**.

When it harbors bitterness, its signal weakens. When it releases mercy, its power multiplies.

Forgiveness is therefore not optional—it is the maintenance system of divine power.

Let us trace the process in four progressive movements:

1. Acknowledge the Wound Without Judgment

The Spirit cannot heal what you hide.

Name the pain, but refuse to rehearse the blame.

Say: "Father, this hurt me, but I choose to see it through Your eyes."

Acknowledgment opens the door; judgment closes it.

2. Invite the Spirit Into the Memory

Imagine that event bathed in golden light.

See the presence of Jesus standing within that moment.

Where there was betrayal, see His compassion.

Where there was silence, hear His whisper: *"I was there."*

His presence rewrites the memory's frequency from trauma to testimony.

3. Release the Emotional Charge

Exhale deeply and speak aloud: "I release them. I release myself."

Feel the weight leave your chest.

The Holy Spirit often moves through breath; every exhale is surrender, every inhale is renewal.

As you breathe forgiveness, your cells receive life.

4. Replace Pain With Purpose

Ask, *"What divine strength was born from this?"*

Every wound, once healed, becomes a portal of wisdom.

Forgiveness transforms pain into power and memory into ministry.

When you complete this process, your heart's energy field expands dramatically.

You may sense warmth, lightness, or even tears of relief.

These are not emotions alone—they are **signals of restored flow**.

Heaven recognizes the resonance of a forgiven heart.

Angels respond. Miracles align. Relationships realign.

You are no longer anchored to yesterday; you are available for tomorrow.

Forgiveness also reconnects you to compassion.

Those who wounded you often operated from their own brokenness.

When you forgive, you stop mirroring their pain and start reflecting God's love.

You cease being a reactive soul and become a redemptive spirit.

Living in the Energy of Ongoing Forgiveness

True freedom comes when forgiveness becomes a **lifestyle, not an event**.

Daily release keeps your heart clear and your energy bright.

- Forgive *quickly*, before resentment takes root.
- Forgive *freely*, without expecting repayment.
- Forgive *fully*, allowing love to fill the space once occupied by hurt.

Make forgiveness a morning ritual. Before you face the world, whisper,

"Lord, I release all yesterday's burdens. I enter this day light and free."

Your heart will thank you.

Your mind will quiet.

Your body will heal faster.

Your relationships will breathe again.

Forgiveness is not only a moral command—it is *vibrational hygiene*.

End-of-Chapter Framework

Self-Reflection Questions

1. What past wound still replays in my thoughts or emotions?
2. How might my unforgiveness be restricting the flow of peace and provision in my life?
3. Who do I need to release today so that my energy aligns again with divine grace?

Devotional Insight (Redirected, Readjusted, Set Aright, Increased in Holiness)

The Spirit redirects your gaze from injustice to inner freedom.

He readjusts your heart from resentment to radiant peace.

He sets aright your identity—you are not a victim of pain but a vessel of mercy.

As holiness increases, the flow of divine energy cleanses every cell and restores your joy.

Affirmation of Faith

"My heart is free from offense.

The energy of forgiveness flows through me like living water.

I release the past, bless those who hurt me, and embrace peace as my inheritance.

My heart is clear, my spirit is strong, and my life is open to miracles."

Prayer of Release

Father, thank You for the mercy that has cleansed my soul.

I choose to forgive every person who has wounded me.

I release their debt into Your hands and free myself from judgment.

Wash my memories with light; fill every empty place with love.

Let Your Spirit flow again through my heart without hindrance.

Make me a fountain of forgiveness to others.

In Jesus' name, Amen.

Scripture Anchors

- *Ephesians 4:32* — "Forgive each other, just as in Christ God forgave you."
- *Matthew 6:14-15* — "If you forgive others... your Father will forgive you."
- *Luke 23:34* — "Father, forgive them, for they know not what they do."

Key Takeaways

- Forgiveness restores energetic and spiritual flow.
- Unforgiveness constricts the heart's magnetic field and drains vitality.

- Releasing offense re-aligns you with divine peace and attracts miracles.
- Living in daily forgiveness keeps your atmosphere pure and powerful.

Call to Action

Find a quiet place. Write the names of anyone who still occupies your emotional space.

Beside each, write: *"I release you. I bless you. I am free."*

Then tear or burn the paper as a prophetic act of liberation.

Feel the air lighten, your breath deepen, and your heart expand.

Walk away knowing: the river flows again.

CHAPTER TWENTY

The Heart's Dominion Restored: Walking in Wholeness, Authority, and Light

"Arise, shine; for your light has come, and the glory of the Lord has risen upon you." — Isaiah 60:1 (AMP)

Part A — Revelation and Definition

In the beginning, when God breathed His Spirit into humanity, He crowned the human vessel with dominion — not as domination but as divine partnership. Dominion was never about control; it was about **alignment**. It was the outward expression of inward harmony, the authority that flows naturally when the spirit, mind, and body move in perfect oneness under the rule of divine love.

When Adam fell, that alignment fractured. The human heart, once radiant with unbroken communion, dimmed under the weight of separation. Fear replaced faith. Effort replaced flow. Humanity began to live *from the outside in* — reacting to circumstance instead of radiating from divine center.

But in Christ, dominion is restored. The second Adam does not simply recover what was lost — He re-creates humanity into a higher frequency of divine expression. The Kingdom within you is the re-emergence of that original design: **Spirit ruling through the heart, illuminating the mind, and animating the body with divine purpose.**

To walk in dominion, therefore, is not to strive for control but to *surrender to coherence*.

It is to let the Spirit reign from the heart outward until every thought, cell, and action harmonizes with heaven.

The Threefold Restoration

1. **Restoration of Identity — Spirit Awakens**
   Dominion begins with remembrance: you are not flesh trying to become spiritual; you are spirit temporarily expressed through flesh. When identity shifts from survival to sonship, the Spirit re-takes the throne of inner governance.

2. **Restoration of Consciousness — Mind Renewed**
   The renewed mind becomes translator between heaven and earth. As the mind yields to truth, it stops echoing fear and starts interpreting revelation. You think as God thinks — creatively, compassionately, courageously.

3. **Restoration of Embodiment — Body Anointed**
   The body, once burdened by stress and shame, becomes a temple of radiance. Every heartbeat carries worship; every movement becomes ministry. You live as walking sanctuary — the Word made flesh again through yielded life.

The Law of Inner Government

The heart's dominion operates through spiritual law:

- The **Spirit** governs by revelation.
- The **Heart** executes through love.

- The **Mind** manages through understanding.
- The **Body** manifests through obedience.

When these four dimensions are synchronized, divine authority flows without interruption.

You no longer "command" by emotion but by **alignment** — your decree carries weight because heaven recognizes itself in your vibration.

This is what Jesus demonstrated. Every miracle He performed was an act of inner government — peace within commanding chaos without. When the storm raged, His heart was still; when death loomed, His Spirit spoke life. He ruled not by resistance but by resonance.

Dominion, therefore, is the state of perfect **agreement** between heaven's order and your internal reality.

The Radiance of Wholeness

A heart in dominion radiates peace.

A mind in submission reflects wisdom.

A body in alignment releases healing.

Together, they form the image of divine light — the visible evidence that God lives within.

This radiance is not symbolic. It is literal spiritual energy. When your entire being moves in harmony with love, you emit the electromagnetic signature of glory. The environment responds — disorder bends toward order; decay yields to life; brokenness dissolves in presence.

That is Kingdom dominion manifested — *not by might, nor by power, but by My Spirit,* says the Lord.

Dominion as Divine Flow

To walk in dominion is to live in *continuous circulation* of God's power:

1. **Receive** from the Spirit.
2. **Release** through the heart.
3. **Renew** in worship.
4. **Re-enter** the world carrying His frequency.

This rhythmic exchange keeps the believer fresh, creative, and unafraid. Dominion is dynamic, never stagnant — it breathes, expands, and transforms every environment it touches.

Restored Dominion in Daily Life

- When you speak from peace, your words carry creation power.
- When you serve from compassion, you multiply resources.
- When you walk in joy, you heal atmospheres without trying.
- When you forgive, you disarm darkness.
- When you worship, you govern realms unseen.

Dominion is lived, not announced. It is the quiet authority of one who has returned to wholeness — spirit, mind, and body functioning as one divine instrument.

In this restoration, *The Heart's Dominion* is not merely theological; it is experiential. You become the living continuation of Eden — a sanctuary in motion, a field of light through which heaven continually expresses itself on earth.

Part B — Kingdom Insight and Application

Dominion is not theory—it's demonstration. It is the day-to-day embodiment of heaven's government through a yielded life. The believer whose heart, mind, and body are synchronized with the Spirit becomes a living embassy of the Kingdom.

1. Walking in Restored Authority

Authority is not volume; it is vibration. When your inner frequency resonates with God's Word, creation recognizes its original language. Mountains move because they hear the tone of their Creator again—spoken now through you.

Every decision made from peace carries weight. You no longer speak *to* situations; you speak *from* divine position. Prayer becomes decree, and obedience becomes propulsion. Dominion, then, is the calm confidence that heaven backs what love commands.

2. The Discipline of Inner Stillness

To rule outwardly, you must be governed inwardly. The soul that learns stillness becomes a throne of presence. In stillness, revelation ripens. In silence, wisdom speaks.

Practice pausing before every response—breathe once for heaven. Let each breath remind you that rulership flows from rest. When your pulse slows to God's rhythm, discernment sharpens, and your words begin to create rather than react.

3. Recalibrating the Mind to Kingdom Logic

The renewed mind interprets from Spirit, not from scarcity. It measures possibility by divine supply, not human probability.

To walk in dominion is to think redemptively: seeing potential where others see problems.

Each morning, ask:

"How would heaven think about this day?"

Then act accordingly. You will notice divine coincidences—doors opening, favor aligning—because your mental atmosphere now harmonizes with God's intent.

4. Embodying Divine Health and Presence

The body is not the servant of sin but the sanctuary of glory. Treat it as such. Rest when Spirit instructs. Feed it life-giving words and food. Move with gratitude.

Every physical act can be an act of worship—stretching becomes prayer, walking becomes procession, breathing becomes intercession. As the body obeys the rhythm of heaven, it emits peace that heals others without touch.

5. Practicing Dominion in Relationships

Authority divorced from compassion becomes control; love without boundaries becomes chaos. Kingdom dominion is the balance of both—truth held in tenderness.

In conversation, choose understanding over winning. In leadership, choose service over spotlight. In conflict, be the stable center. Your calm will shift rooms faster than arguments ever could.

6. The Currency of Joy

Joy is spiritual voltage—the evidence that divine energy is flowing freely. A joyless believer is an unplugged believer. Joy announces confidence in God's sovereignty and keeps the heart magnetic to miracles.

Protect your joy like treasure. Sing often. Laugh with heaven. Refuse heaviness. Joy is not denial—it is dominion expressed as delight.

7. Living as Light in Motion

The ultimate proof of restored dominion is illumination. You carry light wherever you go, and darkness yields automatically. Your presence becomes prophetic atmosphere—homes calm, hearts soften, minds awaken.

You need not advertise light; it reveals itself. Simply remain transparent before God. The clearer the vessel, the brighter the shine.

Seven Focus Points for Expansion

The Next Dimensions of The Heart's Dominion

1. The Architecture of Divine Coherence

Theology: God designed the human vessel as a triune architecture—spirit, mind, and body—mirroring His own nature. When these three align, the individual becomes an echo of divine harmony.

Kingdom Insight: Coherence is the signature of the Kingdom; disorder signals distance from divine rhythm. The more unified your inner world, the greater your outer influence.

Practical Activation: Teach readers how to cultivate daily coherence through breath prayer, worship stillness, and gratitude journaling—bringing the nervous system, thoughts, and spirit into one holy pulse.

2. The Frequency of Glory

Theology: Glory is not merely light—it is the measurable energy of God's presence. Every act of holiness amplifies that frequency.

Kingdom Insight: Living in continual worship expands the believer's field of light until environments shift and healing becomes natural.

Practical Activation: Lead believers into "glory immersion"—five minutes of heart-centered worship where they visualize light expanding outward. Record testimonies of atmosphere change, reconciliation, or physical renewal.

3. The Law of Inner Government

Theology: Dominion operates by divine order: Spirit governs, heart executes, mind interprets, and body manifests. This hierarchy reflects heaven's government within man.

Kingdom Insight: Many lose authority because their inner government is inverted—emotion commanding spirit. Restoration begins when divine order returns.

Practical Activation: Develop daily declarations of hierarchy: *"My spirit leads, my heart loves, my mind agrees, my body obeys."* Include a guided practice for resetting inner order when confusion arises.

4. The Science of Faith Energy

Theology: Faith is spiritual energy converted into substance through belief. Hebrews 11:1 describes it as both *substance* and *evidence*—spiritual materialization in motion.

Kingdom Insight: Faith operates like light: invisible until it strikes resistance, then revealed through manifestation.

Practical Activation: Teach believers to measure their "faith energy" through emotional indicators—peace, expectation, joy—and to recalibrate by worship when those drop. Combine biblical meditation with physiological awareness.

5. The Heart's Electromagnetic Covenant

Theology: The heart's field extends several feet beyond the body, symbolizing covenant connection between heaven and humanity.

Kingdom Insight: When two believers in unity pray, their fields synchronize—creating exponential amplification of divine energy.

Practical Activation: Form "Covenant Circles" for intercession. Members align their hearts in forgiveness first, then declare one unified prayer. Teach this as a model for corporate dominion and healing ministry.

6. The Path of Regenerative Holiness

Theology: Holiness is not abstention—it is regeneration. It restores divine order, renews cellular integrity, and purifies thought patterns.

Kingdom Insight: Every act of holiness increases vibrational clarity, allowing the Spirit's power to flow unimpeded through the vessel.

Practical Activation: Encourage believers to practice *holiness hygiene*—intentional detox from negative media, toxic conversation, and inner criticism—while infusing time with worship, Scripture, and rest.

7. The Ministry of Radiant Presence

Theology: The mature believer becomes a living sacrament—God seen through human form. Presence itself becomes ministry.

Kingdom Insight: When the spirit rules, your very presence preaches. Without speaking, you shift atmospheres and awaken faith in others.

Practical Activation: Create training for "Presence Evangelism." Before meetings or ministry moments, participants pause, breathe, and silently invite the Spirit to radiate through them—ministering beyond words.

These seven focus points form the blueprint for the **next phase** of *The Heart's Dominion*—a multidimensional discipleship system uniting revelation, neuroscience, spiritual formation, and practical transformation.

End-of-Chapter Framework

Self-Reflection Questions

1. Which area of my being—spirit, mind, or body—still struggles to submit fully to divine harmony?
2. How have I used control instead of communion when exercising authority?
3. Where can I embody more light and peace in my daily environment?
4. What does dominion look like in my relationships, my decisions, and my service?
5. How will I commit to living as a walking sanctuary of glory every day?

Devotional Insight (Redirected, Readjusted, Set Aright, Increased in Holiness)

The Spirit redirects your focus from achievement to alignment.

He readjusts your inner atmosphere until peace becomes your natural state.

He sets aright every fragmented thought so that revelation flows unhindered.

As holiness increases, dominion ceases to be a task and becomes your nature— effortless authority born from perfect agreement with God.

Affirmation of Faith

"My spirit rules under the government of God.

My heart is pure, my mind is renewed, my body is strong.

I walk in divine order and release heaven's peace wherever I go.

The glory within me expands daily, transforming everything I touch.

I live, move, and have my being in perfect union with the Spirit of God."

Prayer of Dominion and Dedication

Father of Glory,

I thank You for restoring the dominion of my heart.

Let Your Spirit reign within me without resistance.

Every thought, emotion, and action I surrender to Your rhythm.

Teach me to govern from peace, to speak from wisdom, to move in love.

Make me a living reflection of heaven's order on earth.

Let the light of Christ radiate from me—healing, reconciling, awakening.

May my life be a continual act of worship and authority in Your name.

Amen.

Scripture Anchors

- *Isaiah 60:1* — "Arise, shine; for your light has come."
- *Romans 5:17* — "Those who receive abundance of grace… will reign in life through the One, Jesus Christ."

- *1 Thessalonians 5:23* — "May your whole spirit, soul, and body be preserved blameless."
- *John 17:22* — "The glory which You gave Me I have given them."

Key Takeaways

- Dominion is divine coherence—spirit, mind, and body in perfect alignment.
- Authority flows from peace, not force; from inner order, not outer control.
- Every believer carries the electromagnetic signature of God's glory.
- Wholeness and holiness are inseparable; one sustains the other.
- Living in continual communion keeps your dominion active and expanding.

Call to Action

1. Begin each day by declaring: *"The Kingdom within me governs my world today."*
2. Spend five minutes aligning breath, thought, and spirit—three slow inhales of gratitude, three exhales of surrender.
3. Throughout the day, practice silent awareness of God's presence in your heart.
4. Before sleep, thank Him for the day's flow of authority and peace. These daily rhythms transform dominion from concept to

lifestyle—until you no longer try to walk in power; you simply **are** power revealed.

Benediction and Final Blessing

Beloved, you were created to shine.
From the first breath of creation, God's Spirit ordained that your heart would be His dwelling place—His throne within flesh, His light within clay.

Now walk as one who remembers.
Let every step announce peace.
Let every word carry healing.
Let every glance release hope.

May your heart remain the sanctuary of divine presence—
your mind the mirror of divine wisdom,
your body the instrument of divine purpose.

May your atmosphere be filled with the fragrance of glory,
and may those who cross your path sense the nearness of heaven.

The Lord bless you with clarity of spirit,
strength of purpose,
and stability of peace.
The Lord cause His light to flow through you like living fire,
purifying and empowering every dimension of your being.

Go forth as a carrier of Kingdom dominion—
not striving, but shining;
not controlling, but creating;
not surviving, but ruling through love.

And when the world sees your light,
may they glorify your Father in heaven.

Amen. Selah.

www.ingramcontent.com/pod-product-compliance
Lightning Source LLC
Chambersburg PA
CBHW071215160426
43196CB00012B/2305